The Churches of the West

/ A SUN BOOK

The Churches of the West

by MARCEL PACAUT

Agrégé de l'Université

/ A SUN BOOK

Translated by Bernard Denvir

Walker and Company, NEW YORK

Preface

This book is intended as a guide to the structure of the various church organizations of modern Western Europe, with some reference to their historical evolution. It does not attempt either to discuss doctrine or to make any comparative evaluations. It is hoped that it will prove a useful foundation for students interested in the subject. For further reading a short bibliography has been added. It should provide more detailed analyses of the various aspects mentioned briefly in the text.

As far as possible the facts and figures are the most recent available.

Contents

Part One / The Roman Catholic Church

Part Two / The Protestant Churches

Part Three / Judaism and the Orthodox Church

Part One
The Roman Catholic Church

1 / The Pope and the Cardinals

The structure of the Roman Catholic Church is a hierarchy at the head of which is the pope, who is at the head of all clergy and the general body of the faithful. He is surrounded by counselors whom he chooses himself, of whom the most important are the cardinals.

The Pope

The Roman Primacy. This sovereign power, however, was not always acknowledged as residing in the Sovereign Pontiff. On the contrary, in the early days of Christianity the pope was merely the bishop of Rome. But this see, the capital of the Empire, naturally enjoyed a certain pre-eminence. Only in the ninth century did the concept of the primacy of Rome over the rest of the Church begin to appear clearly in canon law. Then, in the course of the Middle Ages, the papacy, profiting from the struggle it carried on against temporal sovereigns to prevent lay intervention in spiritual matters, established its own omnipotence, and created those elements of a centralized administrative bureaucracy that reached their apogee in the middle of the thirteenth and the early decades of the fourteenth century. This period also saw the Great Schism (1378–1418) —a grave crisis that produced the conciliar theory, according to which an Ecumenical Council (one was held in 1962) is superior in power to the pope. This involved the papacy in another struggle—one made all the more difficult by the grave administrative abuses that were then provoking violent criticism. This criticism provoked the Protestant Reformation, which itself led to a return to a stricter discipline—formulated by the Council of Trent (1545–1563), at which the primacy of Rome was once again defined. Then came a movement toward the establishment of national churches (Gallicanism in France, Anglicanism in England). However, this movement gradually decreased in vigor between the seventeenth and nineteenth centuries, at the end of which period the papacy was able once again to regain its omnipotence, solemnly proclaimed at the Vatican Council of 1870.

According to the canons of this Council (in which were incorporated many earlier texts) the power of the Holy Father comes directly from God. The pope is above all bishops, who are themselves the successors of the apostles to whom Jesus gave the power to bind and loose. (Peter received a mission to "feed my lambs, feed my sheep," and had conferred on him a special pre-eminence, by virtue of the celebrated text "Thou art Peter, and upon this rock I shall build my Church.") The pope is therefore the successor of St. Peter and the head of the whole Church, the living representative of Christ on earth.

This primacy, however, does not consist in a negation of all inferior jurisdictions, but in a limitless power of control over the functioning of all ecclesiastical courts and administrative organs. In practice, this gives the pope omnipotence, limited only by his own interpretations of this omnipotence. Catholics believe that it is only by reason of this primacy that "the necessary doctrinal and administrative unity that are the essentials of Catholicism" can be preserved. Finally, this primacy belongs to the Bishop of Rome because, by a special dispensation of Providence, Peter decided to establish his own see in Rome. But the pope is not absolutely bound to reside in Rome, and no theological rule or act of canon law prevents him from establishing his seat elsewhere.

Papal Infallibility. The Vatican Council also enunciated the doctrine of papal infallibility. This, according to its decrees, "stems from that Divine Providence which forever shields the see of Peter and its holders from all possibility of error." But only those acts that the pope performs in the plenitude of his apostolic power are considered

infallible—that is, those that come from the pope himself
(for a council is not infallible) and that have as their
province "to define a doctrine concerned with faith or
morals."

The conditions that confer infallibility on a papal decision are therefore very sharply defined. We might say
that the most important of them is that any such pronounce-
ment must be *ex cathedra*—from the heights of the Chair
of Peter—a stipulation that insures that any such state-
ment will spring from the papal function of teaching the
truth. No special solemnity is necessary for such teaching—
the pope has merely to state that what he is proclaiming
is "a dogma binding on all the faithful." It must be a doctrine that springs from a revealed truth or one related to
revelation, and also one that has already been defined or admitted by the Church. It is therefore only on very rare
occasions that popes have conferred infallibility on their
pronouncements. Contrary to general belief, encyclicals
(letters addressed by the pope to the entire world, like the
recent *Mater et Magistra,* which is largely concerned with
economic matters) do not necessarily impart infallible
teachings—that is, they do not consist of a body of beliefs
automatically binding upon the faithful. To make them
such, the pope must expressly so define them.

The Papal Election; The Conclave. It is easy to
understand, in view of the extraordinary powers he possesses, the care the Church takes over the choice of a pope.
Nevertheless, papal elections have not always followed the

pattern they do now. For many centuries the choice of the pope belonged exclusively to the clergy and laity of Rome, who chose him in much the same fashion as the churches of any other great city would choose their own bishop. This led to grave abuses and an outcrop of scandals, the papacy becoming no more than an office at the disposal of the head of the Holy Roman Empire, or a pawn to be played for by the members of the Roman aristocracy. By the beginning of the eleventh century the popes had begun to take steps to rescue the papacy from the mercy of the temporal powers, and to avert schisms. In the course of time, therefore, several enactments were issued to define the conditions for holding papal elections. Five are particularly important: the decree of Nicholas II in 1059, which confined the election to the body of cardinals, giving a special role to the cardinal bishops; the canon of the Third Lateran Council, promulgated in 1179 by Alexander III, which stipulated that the pope had to be elected by a majority of two-thirds of the cardinals; the canon of the Third Council of Lyons (1274), which fixed the regulations for the conclave; the two bulls of Gregory XV (1621 and 1622), which established the procedure for the scrutiny of the votes; and the constitution of Pius X, in 1904, which recapitulated all these earlier regulations and stipulated conditions of absolute freedom and secrecy for the election. Since then there have been no further changes.

On the death of the pope those cardinals who are in residence in the city when the death takes place wait ten days for the arrival of their absent colleagues. At the end of this interval they meet, usually in a part of the Vatican specially prepared for the purpose. No cardinal is allowed more than two servants. They are then closed up in the section of the building reserved for them, and are forced to live in common, each having only a cell for sleeping. No one may communicate with them, and their food is passed to them through a hatch specially made for that purpose. This cloistral seclusion for the election of a pope is known as the *conclave*. The Cardinal Camerlingo (or Chamberlain) of the Holy Roman Church, who is in charge of the temporal administration of the Holy See during the vacancy, oversees the meticulous observation of these rules, with the assistance of a council composed of the senior cardinals.

Once shut up (if by chance a cardinal has to leave the conclave, he is not allowed to return) the cardinals are not allowed to discuss anything but the election of the new pope. They vote twice a day—once in the morning, once in the evening—the rest of the time being occupied with prayer, and with conversations aimed at bringing about an election as quickly as possible. Indeed they go on voting until the requisite two-thirds majority is obtained. If at the end of three days they have not been successful, their food ration is reduced, a procedure that is repeated at the end of another five days.

These stipulations, however, have not always succeeded in shortening conclaves. (That of 1800 took three months.)

In part this is because the method of scrutiny—laid down in 1621–22—is very strict. Three methods are allowed: by acclamation; by delegation (the cardinals entrusting the election to a select number from their own ranks); and by secret scrutiny. Only this last method is now used. Each cardinal writes his own name and that of the person he has chosen on a ballot that he places in the urn, after taking an oath that he is voting for the one whom he thinks most worthy of election. (All prior "understandings" are forbidden under pain of excommunication.) The three Cardinals Scrutator, chosen by lot, then count the ballots. As we have noted, a two-thirds majority is necessary for election, but if a cardinal votes for himself his vote is void. (For this reason the name of the voter is hidden from the scrutinizing cardinals as they unfold the ballots; they verify it only if one candidate should obtain exactly two-thirds of the votes.) Then, to expedite results, after each unfolding of the ballots those cardinals who have not voted for a candidate who is only a few votes short of the requisite majority may change their votes to give him the necessary number—a process known as "accession." At the end of each scrutiny the ballots are burned, and the cardinals swear that they will not disclose what has taken place within the conclave.

Once elected the pope has to accept his nomination and choose the name by which he will be known. Thenceforth he is pope; the insignia of his office are conferred on him some days later when he is consecrated by the cardinal bishop of Ostia. Let us note, however, that the cardinals are not obliged to elect one of their own number, but may choose anyone they please—even a layman. (In such a case, the person elected must be ordained a priest before he is consecrated.) But, as soon as he accepts his nomination, the new pope is the head of the entire Church, and the cardinals immediately pay homage to him. He is, however, permitted to resign during his pontificate, and his resignation cannot be refused.

The Cardinals

Their Origin. In the early centuries of the Church the title *"cardinal"* (*incardinatus*) was given to certain clergy who, by virtue of their functions, were especially attached to the service of a church. They were the "hinges" of that church; hence their name, *cardo.* Further, since Rome was the main center of Christianity, the bishop of Rome gradually gathered around him a large number of ecclesiastics. He needed deacons, for instance, to distribute alms in the seven deaconries created by Pope Fabian. In the same way, certain "cardinals" were specially entrusted with the direction and organization of religious services in the Roman parishes. Moreover, the popes acquired the custom of holding regular meetings with the bishops of those sees that neighbored on Rome—Ostia, Porto, Santo-Ruffino, Albano, Tusculum, Preneste and Sabina—and of asking their advice whenever important decisions had to be taken. Gradually the *incardinati* of the various churches disappeared, their places being taken by the "cardinals" of the Church, counselors-in-ordinary to the pope, who confided special duties to them. But it was not till later, in the twelfth and thirteenth centuries, that the cardinals became a formal body—which has since come to be called the Sacred College—presided over by a dean, a camerlingo and a secretary. Still more recently their number was fixed at seventy: six cardinal bishops, fifty cardinal priests and fourteen cardinal deacons.[1] However, the pope can always modify these numbers if he sees fit. In actuality the full number of seventy, fixed in the sixteenth century by Sixtus V, has never been completely filled.

All the cardinals participate in the general administration and direction of the Church, but the cardinal bishops are also the ordinaries of the "suburbanical" diocese that they actually control. The cardinal priests, however, have little or nothing to do with the particular Roman parish whose title they bear, though they are bishops of dioceses in other parts of the world. No hard and fast rule determines the distribution in national terms of the various cardinals, nor are they necessarily attached to one see. Finally, the cardinal deacons are entrusted specially with the day-to-day running of the Church. The Sacred College is always presided over by a dean, who is, as far as circumstances permit, the cardinal bishop of Ostia. Many members

[1] In 1960 Pope John XXIII fixed the College of Cardinals at 74. —Tr.

of the College are concerned with the running of the various administrative services and the congregations of the Roman Curia itself.

The Appointment of Cardinals. Only the pope can appoint a cardinal, and though he usually asks the advice of the Sacred College, he is not bound by it. The qualities demanded of a candidate reflect on his piety, the austerity of his life, and his intellectual caliber. Theoretically, no relation of a living cardinal can be nominated;[2] nor can anyone who has had children—even from a legitimate marriage contracted before taking holy orders. At present —although the example of Cardinal Mazarin proves that the rule has not always been in force—a man must be a priest before he can become a cardinal.

The Holy See, however, in view of the prestige conferred on its incumbent, has adopted the habit of conferring a cardinal's hat only after consultation with the government of the country to which the candidate belongs. This is only a custom, made necessary by current political conditions; it is in no sense obligatory.

The new cardinal having received notification of his nomination, the pope confers on him the insignia of his office, at a private ceremony in the presence of those cardinals resident in the Vatican at the time. These insignia are the biretta and the red hat, which the pope places on

2 Nevertheless there are at present two brothers—named Cicognani—in the Sacred College. Cf. *The Times* (London), August 15, 1961, page 6.—TR.

the new cardinal's head, at the same time slipping on his finger a sapphire ring, and conferring on him his title. Then the pope opens and closes his mouth, showing thereby that he places complete trust in the new cardinal's counsel and discretion.

The Role of the Cardinals. Since the thirteenth century cardinals have been the leading ecclesiastical dignitaries after the Sovereign Pontiff, to whom they always have free access. According to protocol they have the rank of princes, a fact that enhances their prestige still further. At councils of the Church they are the first to give their advice to the pope.

The role they actually play is, however, much more precise than this. It consists in participating in papal elections, administering those dioceses of which they are the titular heads, and directing those administrative services of the Church that are in their charge. Above all, the cardinals are the permanent advisers of the pope. True, he is not bound to ask their advice, or to follow it when it is given; and many popes, from inclination or policy, have preferred to keep their own counsel in making decisions, or to ask the advice of those in humbler positions, holding less exalted posts in the ecclesiastical hierarchy. However, the importance of the cardinals' position is not affected by the personality of the Sovereign Pontiff.

Those cardinals who are in charge of dioceses or provinces acquire immense influence in their own countries, and the spiritual and religious role they play is of the greatest importance. If we add to this the independence conferred on them by their title of Prince of the Church, and the universal nature of the Church they represent, it is easy to understand something of the semipolitical importance of their position. To raise a hand against a cardinal is to attack the Church itself, since the cardinalate is an essentially Roman dignity, conferring on its holder a part in the general government of the Church. And those who live permanently in Rome, presiding over one or another of the various religious or administrative bodies of the papacy, also play a major role, since they are the highest Roman officials and the immediate executants of papal mandates.

From time to time the pope calls together an assembly both of the cardinals resident in Rome and those outside the Eternal City; this is known as a *consistory*. Some of these meetings are public, but if such they are little more than diplomatic occasions, and numerous prelates and political personalities are also invited. Other consistories are held in secret; their purpose is to formulate certain decisions that the pope must make. From the beginning of the thirteenth century, when they first began to appear, consistories increased in frequency as ecclesiastical tradition tended toward the theory that all important decisions affecting the Church should be taken by meetings rather than by individuals. In our own time, however, the pope rarely summons a consistory, but rather seeks the advice of the cardinals by direct consultation, and then proclaims his decision in the presence of those who happen to be in Rome at that particular moment. Even so, however, there are still occasions on which he actually takes decisions "in consistory."

Such, then, is the way in which the Sovereign Pontiff, and under his absolute authority, the various branches of the ecclesiastical civil service, usually presided over by a cardinal, direct the policy, government and administration of the Church.

2 / The Government of the Church: The Roman Curia

The government and administration of the Roman Catholic Church are confided to the Curia. Originally this consisted of those clergy and prelates who were in the immediate entourage of the pope; and apart from a few administrative organs such as the Chancellory and the Treasury it was not formally organized. From the beginning of the sixteenth century on, permanent commissions (known as "Congregations") were set up; after several changes, their general organization has remained as fixed by Pius X in 1908. The Curia is made up of these congregations, and also of various tribunals and offices. Each of these bodies has the generic name *dicasterum,* and is solely responsible for those matters that come within its province. If there is a conflict of authority with another body, the pope nominates a commission of cardinals to decide the matter. Aside from this, the competence of the *dicastera* does not stop with the death of the pope, and they are in fact the basic elements of Roman government. Their members, moreover, are bound to secrecy about their deliberations and the work they do. Also, the pope has, and always has had, special means of acting on his own, quite apart from the Curia.

The Exercise of Papal Power

Its Nature. The Roman primacy is translated into executive action through the pope's power of supreme jurisdiction—a power described in canon law as "entire, universal, truly episcopal, ordinary and direct." It is expressed in the symbols of authority special to the papacy: the tiara with its three crowns, the pallium, the papal cross, the Fisherman's Ring, and so on.

Furthermore, the pope is also a sovereign on the international plane. He depends on no external political power, and recognizes no such power as having any authority over his person, goods or entourage; nor does he pay any customs dues or receive any subsidy. All these prerogatives have been meticulously laid down and defined in the concordats that the Holy See has signed with various governments, and especially with that of Italy. The struggle for Italian unity resulted—in 1870—in the papacy's being deprived of the lands it had controlled since the eighth century. For nearly sixty years after 1870 the popes considered themselves prisoners within the Vatican, a situation that only came to an end with the Lateran Treaty of 1929. Since that date the papacy has recovered its territorial integrity, in the form of the Vatican City and certain outlying possessions, over which the pope exercises the power of a temporal sovereign.

In this capacity the pope controls an organization that includes various prelates, prothonotaries, chamberlains, chaplains and lay employees, as well as several military bodies, including the Noble Guard, composed of members of the Roman aristocracy who provide an escort for the pope when he leaves his apartments; the Swiss Guard, which is responsible for his protection; the Palatine Guard of Honor, a purely ceremonial body; and the Papal Gendarmes, who look after the security of the papal buildings. Together these comprise a strictly temporal and localized group of institutions, having no connection with the spiritual and ecclesiastical powers, which are the concern not only of the Curia but of church councils and legates.

Councils and Legates. When the Roman Catholic Church has to make important decisions—or at any time the pope sees fit—he can summon an *Ecumenical Council.* This is a convocation of cardinals, patriarchs, primates, archbishops, diocesan bishops and those abbots who are heads of religious congregations, as well as other prelates and theologians, according to the specific needs of the Council. Only the pope can summon a Council, and he can bring its deliberations to an end whenever he wants. In the fifteenth century the Councils proclaimed that their authority was superior to that of the pope, but since that time papal pronouncements have branded such a belief suspect of heresy, and in actuality any decision a Council may make must be confirmed and promulgated by the pope.

A Council is not, therefore, an administrative organ, but an assembly that, by virtue of its prestige and moral power, can participate in the ecclesiastical and political government of the Catholic world. Subject to the pope, it serves as a consultative body for him in the exercise of his supreme jurisdiction. Occurring frequently up to the sixteenth century, Councils have been infrequent since. Nevertheless, all the most important decisions in the history of the Church have been their work.[1] The perfecting of the organs of the Curia, the now universally recognized power of the papacy, and purely material difficulties have all tended to make the summoning of Councils less frequent.

Another institution that over the centuries has helped the popes exercise their power over the Church has been that of *legates*. These may be legates *a latere* (that is, sent from the "side" of the pope). If such, they are entrusted with special missions (for which they are endowed with

---

[1] Apart from the very early Councils, at which the main doctrines of the Church evolved, the more important ones include those of the Lateran (1179 and 1215), Lyons (1274), Constance (1414–1418), Trent (1545–1563) and the Vatican (1870). As of this writing, another Council has been summoned by Pope John XXIII for 1962.—TR.

certain specific powers) and are usually cardinals; they fulfill their tasks by virtue of special papal authority delegated to them. *Nuncios*, on the other hand, are legates who are entrusted with a permanent, residential diplomatic mission; in countries in which the government is not Catholic they are known as *internuncios*. Apart from their political task of fostering good relations between the papacy and the country in which they are located, nuncios also keep an eye on the state of the Church in that country, and keep the Vatican informed about this. Usually they are only bishops, but it is easy to understand how important their function is, since they are directly concerned with the government of the Church. The function of the various organs of the Curia, on the other hand, is purely administrative.

The Congregations

Their Characteristics. The congregations are permanent groups charged with the supreme administrative control of ecclesiastical affairs. Certain of them are presided over by the pope himself; others by a cardinal, who bears the title of Prefect. The size of congregations varies. The cardinals (who alone bear the title of Prefect) are assisted by prelates—high religious officials—and a permanent secretary. The pope nominates the cardinals to each congregation, as well as the chief officers; the lesser officials are chosen by competitive examination. Each congregation also nominates "consultors," who give specialized advice when the occasion demands.

The congregations' general functions are judicial and administrative. Specific problems are put to them, on which they give definitive decisions. Any member of the faithful can address himself to any congregation, either directly or through an agent (such as an ecclesiastical lawyer). A bishop may do the same, either for himself or his diocese, or on behalf of a parishioner who confides in him. Finally, there is the right of appeal from a bishop to a congregation; such an appeal is known as a "supplication."

When such a document arrives at its destination any one of several courses may be taken. If the matter is a simple one, minor officials draw up a rescript, which is submitted to the Prefect for his signature. If the matter is more complicated, the superior officers of the congregation (who meet for this purpose several times a week) draw up the rescript. If they feel that the question is a very delicate one, a precis of it is printed and a copy sent to each cardinal member of the congregation, at least ten days before the usual monthly meeting of all the cardinals in Rome. At this meeting an official of the congregation explains the salient points of the problem, and proffers his expert advice; the cardinals then vote, and the majority decision is promulgated. If the matter is of special importance, it is submitted to the pope.

This same process is followed even when a rescript

may have universal significance. However, the decrees of a congregation are not considered infallible—even when promulgated by the pope—unless he makes a special proviso to that effect. These decrees exact from the faithful an "internal assent."

The Various Congregations. The most important is the Holy Office, formerly known as the Inquisition. Founded by Paul III in 1542, it is presided over by the pope himself, and includes special consultants, among whom is the Superior General of the Dominican Order. All its members are sworn to a specially binding secrecy, similar to the seal of the confessional. On the whole, the Holy Office does not make decisions about disciplinary matters, but only about dogma. Its competence extends to "all matters pertaining to faith or morals" (Canon 247) and especially to sins of heresy, but its jurisdiction also includes regulations concerning "mixed" (i.e., between a Catholic and a non-Catholic) marriages, and the condemnation of pernicious literature, the Holy Office having absorbed the old Congregation of the Index.

The Congregation for the Propagation of the Faith, founded in 1622, has as its aim to organize and oversee the propagation of the faith among heretics and infidels. Thus it is mainly concerned with the organization and personnel of Catholic missions, and has—especially since the beginning of this century—been one of the most active of the congregations.

The Congregation for Extraordinary Affairs was created by Pius VII in 1814. Largely as the result of a decree of Pius XI in 1925, it has mainly been concerned with the appointment of bishops, and also with giving advice to the secretary of state on matters relating to the relations of the papacy with foreign governments. It comprises the Cardinal Secretary of the Holy Office, the Cardinal Chancellor of the Roman Church, the Cardinal Datary and the Cardinal Secretary of State, who presides over it. Its members are bound to the same secrecy as are those of the Holy Office.

The Congregation of the Eastern Church was founded relatively recently; it began to function under the pontificate of Benedict XV in 1917. Presided over by the pope himself, it is concerned with everything connected with the churches of the Eastern rite, with the exception of the affairs of the Russian Church, which since 1935 has come within the province of extraordinary ecclesiastical affairs. The authority this congregation exercises over the discipline, administration and ritual of these churches equals that of all the other congregations combined.

The Latin liturgy is the province of the Congregation of Rites, set up in 1587. Questions regarding the administration of the sacraments come within the province of the Congregation of Sacramental Discipline, founded in 1908. The Congregation of Ceremonies controls matters of precedence, and that for Religious supervises the members of religious bodies of both sexes who have taken vows, and all those who lead a communal religious life. The Congregation of the Council controls the discipline of the secular clergy and the laity, while that of Seminaries and Universities has supreme control over all educational establishments connected with the Church—seminaries, Catholic faculties and institutes, secondary and elementary schools. Finally, the Consistorial Congregation is in charge of preparing consistories, and more particularly, the control of the constitution and organization of dioceses.

The Tribunals

The history of the papacy is a constant demonstration of how the Sovereign Pontiffs have continuously augmented their power over bishops and councils by the steady enlargement of their judicial competence.

By increasing the possibilities of an appeal to their courts, and by making it impossible for diocesan and metropolitan judges to reject such an appeal, the popes have encouraged the lower clergy to have recourse to them on every sort of matter. Organized in this way since the fourteenth century, the papal judicial system has become quite efficient in its functioning. At present several distinct tribunals form part of the Roman Curia.

The Rota. Even though in our time its role has been considerably reduced, the Rota is still the most celebrated Roman tribunal. In part it is a court of original jurisdiction for diocesan bishops, dioceses and all individuals and corporations depending directly on the Sovereign Pontiff, who can place special cases within its jurisdiction. It is also a court of appeal for all ecclesiastical tribunals all over the world. The judges who comprise it are all priests, and the legal processes it initiates are conducted in a manner similar to that of civil courts (most of its cases being concerned with secular litigation between ecclesiastics). But the procedures it follows are long and complicated, and its importance, once considerable, has subsequently declined greatly.

The Penitentiary and the Apostolic Segnatura. At the beginning of the thirteenth century there began to appear within the Curia clerics specially charged with granting absolution for those serious sins considered to come solely under the power of the pope. This function was eventually confided to a cardinal who came to be known as the Grand Penitentiary. This functionary had under him a tribunal, known as the Penitentiary, which was responsible for all cases connected with personal problems relating to conscience, the religious life of the faithful, and similar matters.

In 1934 Pius XI reorganized the Penitentiary, which now consists of two main branches: the Office of Indulgences, which regulates the granting of indulgences (though the doctrinal aspect is reserved to the Holy Office); and the Tribunal of the Penitentiary. The Cardinal Grand Penitentiary directs both, with the assistance of six major and a host of minor officials. The Tribunal is divided into several sections, which hold frequent meetings. It judges matters of conscience and all cases relating to the spiritual lives of individuals (such as those having to do with mixed marriages, the annulment of vows, and the like). Any member of the faithful can have recourse to its jurisdiction, either directly or anonymously, through a confessor. A bishop, too, can ask the Tribunal to make decisions about matters upon which he is not able to decide himself. The answers of the Penitentiary are given at about the end of a month, in conditions that insure absolute secrecy.

The Supreme Tribunal of the Apostolic Segnatura

This body comprises the Grand Penitentiary, his major officials and the secretary of the Tribunal. It is above all responsible for deciding on questions of unusual delicacy submitted to the Penitentiary. Secondarily, it can decide theoretical matters submitted to the Rota without having to use the complicated processes peculiar to that office, and without the possibility of appeal, for the Rota must authorize all appeals to itself against its decisions. The Supreme Tribunal is, therefore, used more frequently than the Rota.

These two tribunals are staffed by ecclesiastics of varying rank, all of whom are specially skilled in canon law. The judges are not paid, but litigants are expected to defray the cost involved in convoking the court, bringing together the witnesses, copying documents, carrying on necessary correspondence, and so on.

To sum up, the main papal tribunals are the Penitentiary for spiritual matters, the Holy Office for questions relating to dogma and for certain matrimonial cases, and the Rota and Segnatura, which are appeal tribunals for all ecclesiastical courts. The picture would not be complete, however, if we did not add that the pope may, at his discretion, summon a specific case before him and, if he sees fit, order it tried by special judges nominated by himself.

The Offices

The Offices are organs of the Roman Curia that share to some extent the executive power of the pope, whom they assist in the day-to-day tasks of government. They first appeared in the Middle Ages. Generally, they are directed by cardinals nominated by the pope.

The Chancery. During the Middle Ages, at some time before the twelfth century, there appeared in the pope's household an official, not always at first a cardinal, who bore the title of Vice-Chancellor of the Roman Church. He was responsible for the composition and dispatch of letters sent out by the pope.[2] Today the Chancery comprises scribes, notaries and secretaries, at the head of whom is the Cardinal Chancellor of the Roman Church. Its function is

---

[2] These letters were and are known as "bulls" because, from the early days of the Church, they have borne a leaden seal (*bulla plumbi*) attached to a red cord. Until 1898 they were written in a cursive Gothic script, and thus were quite difficult to read. Until the pontificate of Pius X their dating depended on a calendar that put the beginning of the year at the Feast of the Annunciation (March 25). Today, although bulls still bear the leaden seal and are written on parchment, they are penned in a normal script and dated according to current usage.

to register and dispatch bulls concerning the major affairs of the Church, especially the collation of what are known as consistorial benefices—that is, those conferred either in consistory or only by a decree of the Consistorial Congregation (bishoprics, abbacies and other high ecclesiastical offices). According to canon law, a benefice is defined as a sacred office and the right to collect the revenues attached to that office. To confer a benefice is in the first place to confer a religious obligation, and incidentally to provide the material means for fulfilling that obligation. It is not, therefore, as the word would seem to imply, merely a financial benefit. For a long time, however—in France until the concordat of 1801, and in Spain and Italy even today—every sacred office had attached to it financial revenues, usually in the form of rents or tithes. Today these have been largely replaced by the voluntary gifts of the faithful.

The Datary. This office, which first appeared in the fourteenth century, was, like the Chancery, one of the main instruments whereby the Holy See increased its wealth and power, for its responsibility—as its name indicates—was to date and dispatch certain papal enactments, and in so doing it was able to levy stamp duties. Actually, its role is complementary to that of the Chancery. It is charged with examining candidates for non-consistorial benefices, with drawing up and dispatching documents connected with the collation of these benefices, and more generally, with everything relating to such matters. It is presided over by the Cardinal Datary of the Holy Roman Church.

The Apostolic Chamber. In the same way that they displaced part of their responsibilities onto a chancellor, medieval popes, before the twelfth century, entrusted the direction and control of their revenue and their treasury to a *camiera* or chamberlain. Soon, as the revenues of the Holy See (which at this time was a temporal state) became more important, this official gradually collected around him a fair-sized staff, which came to be known collectively as the *camera*—from the room in which the treasury was kept. (A similar development was taking place in England, where the equivalent office was known as the *camera regis.*) By the fourteenth century this had become the most important organ in the government of the Church, and was charged with the administration of the Papal States, and of the many and varied revenues of the Roman Church. These functions it still discharges, but its role has been greatly diminished. Even so, however, the Apostolic Chamber is still concerned with papal finances and with balancing the varying forms of income and expenditure, and to it alone is confided, during the vacancy of the Holy See, all the rights and belongings of the Roman Church. It is presided over by the Cardinal Camerlingo, whose office confers on him a great deal of importance.

The Secretary of State. This was the last of the important papal offices to develop, but it has assumed increasing importance as the papacy has initiated purely political and diplomatic relations with lay governments or non-Catholic countries. The Cardinal Secretary of State, who presides over it, is in some ways the Foreign Minister of the papacy. The Secretariat comprises three sections. The section dealing with Extraordinary Ecclesiastical Affairs is directed by the secretary of the congregation of the same name; it deals with such matters as the nomination of bishops, and negotiations on this subject with governments. The Ordinary Affairs section deals with general subjects. Finally, there is the Briefs section, which draws up the documents so designated (these being papal letters of less importance than bulls).

We must also note two other Offices—the secretariat of Briefs to Princes, and that of Latin Letters, both of which are concerned with composing in Latin the letters confided to them by the pope.

This complex of organs—Congregations, Tribunals and Offices—comprises the main ecclesiastical machinery of the Catholic Church. The numerous staffs engaged on them— and to these must be added those whose work is connected with such less important institutions as schools, colleges, seminaries, archives, libraries and various supply organizations—make the Vatican a veritable beehive of industry and activity. Under the all-embracing power of the pope, these bodies control either the material life of the Roman Church or the functioning of the Universal Church or—and this perhaps to a greater degree than anything else—the spiritual and religious life of the Catholic world. All of them are in direct contact with the metropolitan and diocesan sees of the Church.

3 / Provinces and Archbishops

During the first few centuries of its existence the Catholic
Church had no organization and no hierarchy, but was
directed from certain local centers that thus became focal
points of Christian life, attracting to them large numbers of
the faithful. There was no organization along territorial
lines; disciplinary powers, administrative functions and the
right to define matters of dogma belonged merely to those
people who, for one reason or another, had happened to
acquire them. Very soon, however, limits came to be set to
these powers along geographical lines, making use of the
territorial boundaries of the Roman Empire to define those
of the Church. Thus were formed those territorial divisions
that still function today, while certain churches retain
special characteristics deriving from their history and the
significant part they played in the past.

Ecclesiastical Geography

The Ecclesiastical Province. As it spread through the Roman Empire, Christianity established in each *civitas* a church under the direction of a bishop. Later, when the organization of Christianity was fixed along territorial lines, episcopal jurisdiction was exercised within the limits of the *civitas.* This was the origin of the diocese. The bishops of the more important sees then took the title of archbishop, and soon came to occupy a place in the hierarchy above that of their neighboring bishops. Thus, in the course of the eighth and ninth centuries, was born the *province,* a grouping of dioceses under a metropolitan. This is the largest ecclesiastical unit.

Apart from mission countries and certain regions that are completely heretical, Catholic countries are divided into provinces and dioceses, the latter being still further subdivided. We must also note a few specially circumscribed areas where a prelate, known in canon law as a *prelatus nullius* (bishop of nowhere) exercises jurisdiction over the clergy and faithful; these areas are outside the diocesan organization. Such, for instance, are the areas around certain abbeys. Thus no ecclesiastical subdivision coincides with the borders of a country as such, although as far as possible care is taken to make the limits of dioceses and provinces coincide with political boundaries. For instance, Great Britain has its provinces of Westminster, Birmingham, Liverpool, Cardiff and Glasgow; France, those of Aix, Avignon, Besançon, Bordeaux, Chambéry, Lyons, Paris, Rheims, Rouen and so on (the two provinces of Metz and Strasbourg answering, for political reasons, directly to the Holy See). There are thirty-eight provinces in Italy, eight in Spain, three in Portugal, one in Holland, and one in Belgium. The bishops of the dioceses that comprise the province are known as *suffragans*. The pope alone has the power to fix the limits of all the ecclesiastical divisions —provinces, dioceses, vicariates and apostolic prefectures.

Patriarchs and Primates. Ancient titles of long standing—attached to sees that played important roles in the development of Christianity—still survive. They only confer honorary privileges on those who bear them, and precedence over other bishops. One exception is offered by the oriental patriarchs, who, under the pope, have authority over those churches that do not follow the Roman rite. These patriarchs include those of the Copts (Alexandria), the Greek Melechites (Antioch), the Syrians (Antioch), the Maronites (Antioch), the Chaldeans (Babylon) and the Armenians (Silesia).

On the contrary, however, the patriarchs of the Latin rite are merely the occupants of sees that were once of great importance. This title had been accorded to the bishops of Rome, the popes, at an early date, and also to the bishops of Alexandria and Antioch. In 1215 it was extended to Jerusalem and Constantinople. At the present time the title of patriarch of these cities (with the exception of Rome and Jerusalem) is conferred on bishops who do not live there, and it is also conferred automatically on the holders of certain metropolitan sees, such as those of Venice and Lisbon. A primate has the same kind of superiority that characterizes a metropolitan, and though at one time the title was quite important, it has shown a marked decline since the eleventh century, and now means little more than the possession of certain rights of precedence. This of course does not mean that a primate cannot exercise a very strong influence, and he usually does. The foremost prelate is therefore the metropolitan, who under the pope, the cardinals and the Curia, exercises an effective role in the government of the Church.

Metropolitans and Archbishops

The Metropolitan. This dignitary is the prelate who is in charge of an ecclesiastical province and whose see is described as a metropolitan one. His office used to play a more important role than it now does.

The mere fact of dividing a country into provinces naturally increased the power of those who presided over them, at the expense of the pope, who was thought of merely as the Metropolitan of Rome. Thus, there developed in the ninth century a tendency for the Church to develop along regional and federal lines. From that time on, however, the papacy, anxious to develop its primacy by exercising it directly over bishops and inferior ecclesiastical offices, brought about a considerable diminution of metropolitan authority, confining it as far as possible to mere administration; and it has remained such ever since.

Metropolitans are now known as archbishops, and in practice every metropolitan is an archbishop. There are, however, archbishops who are not metropolitans—those who are at the head of an archbishopric and not a province, and who therefore do not have suffragan bishops under them (such as the archbishop of Lucca, in Italy). Finally, the pope can confer the personal honor of an archbishopric on a bishop without making his see an archbishopric.

Nomination of Archbishops; The Pallium. The pope alone can appoint archbishops, the appointment being made in consistory, or after action by the Consistorial Congregation. At the same time, this form of appointment can follow various patterns, according to the type of archiepiscopal see and the formula set out in the concordat with the government involved. In this case the procedure followed is identical with that followed in episcopal appointments. (Cf. Chapter 4.) If the new archbishop is already a bishop, papal nomination alone is sufficient, but if he has not received the episcopal office he has still to be consecrated. Nevertheless, whatever his previous status he cannot exercise the powers of a metropolitan until he has received the *pallium,* the symbol of his office, and for this he must petition the Sovereign Pontiff.

According to certain authorities, the origin of this symbol is to be found in rights granted to certain prelates by the Roman emperors. But the majority opinion tends to make it a simple ecclesiastical vestment of the type worn by bishops and priests. It is circular in shape, and made of wool, with two dependent rectangular bands of equal length weighted down with pieces of silk-covered lead. Six black crosses are embroidered on it, four on the circle and one on each dependent band. Finally, pins are attached to fix it to the left shoulder and the back and front of the wearer. The wool of the *pallium* is woven by the Benedictine nuns of the convent of Santa Cecilia in Transtevere, who, each January 21, in the church of St. Agnes-Without-the-Walls, present two white lambs to be blessed by the canons of the Lateran, and then take them to the Vatican, where they are blessed again by the pope. The common wool is taken as a sign of humility; the pins and the cross recall the Crucifixion.

The *pallium* is the actual symbol of metropolitan power, and the archbishop who has received it wears it in public on certain feast days specified by the Holy Father. He cannot surrender it to anyone else, nor can he wear it outside his own province. If he is moved from one province to another he is invested with another *pallium*. He is buried in the last one he has received, earlier ones being placed under his head. Other signs also distinguish him from mere bishops: the archiepiscopal cross, which is carried in front of him, and the green and gold cords on his hat.

The Functions of a Metropolitan. These are of two sorts. On the one hand, there is the ordinary jurisdiction of a bishop, which he exercises within his own diocese. On the other, there are the two kinds of authority that he wields over the suffragan bishops of his own province.

The metropolitan holds a permanent and strictly administrative office. His ecclesiastical court, for instance, serves as a court of original jurisdiction for all secular matters pertaining to his suffragans, who, however, have the right to have these cases tried before a special diocesan commission. The metropolitan also affords a court of appeal against judgments handed down by a bishop's court, and has general supervisory powers over all his suffragans. In cases of difficulty, or if there are misdeeds or abuses of any kind, he must inform the pope. Thus he is both a controlling power and a medium whereby power is transmitted from above. But he possesses no powers specifically his own, nor has he any special spiritual authority beyond being able to celebrate pontifical mass in any cathedral within his province, of blessing the people at any such service, and of having his archiepiscopal cross carried in front of him.

The metropolitan also possesses exceptional rights of jurisdiction in very delicate cases, and in a more general way, on any occasion when the local diocesan powers can find no solution for a problem, and yet there is no need to invoke the jurisdiction of the pope. He can, for instance, confer orders in a case in which the bishop concerned refuses to do so; he can make a visitation of a diocese within his province, after consulting the pope, if the bishop does not do so, and in this instance can exercise the powers of his suffragan. In short, he can fulfill any functions of his subordinates that they may refuse to perform.

The power of a metropolitan is therefore more limited than many think. Nevertheless, he exercises a great deal of influence and holds an important position, if only because he is at the summit of regional administration. In plenary or provincial councils, and in those regular meetings of the bishops of one country that are now customary, the role the metropolitan plays confers prestige and importance on his office.

Provincial Councils and Assemblies. For a long time now it has been the practice to hold not only councils that unite in one body representatives of the whole Catholic world, but also assemblies of a more limited kind (popularly known as synods) at which the prelates of one country, region or province meet at regular intervals.

Actually, canon law describes as "plenary councils" all those that group representatives from several provinces. They can only be convoked by the pope, who appoints a legate to preside over them. At these meetings are present the metropolitan archbishops, their suffragans, the *prelati nullii* who come within the territorial boundaries of the area represented by these provinces, and if the occasion demands, the vicars-capitular and the apostolic prefects of the same regions. Members of the lower orders of the clergy may also be invited to attend, but they have only a consultative role. In our time these councils have become extremely rare. The metropolitan, however, is under an obligation to summon, at least every twenty years (according to the current demands of canon law) a meeting of all his suffragans, the *prelati nullii* and representatives of the chapters. These meetings are known as "provincial councils"; they are held to regulate all important matters relative to the activities of the province. Their decisions are sent to the Congregation of the Council, which authorizes them to be promulgated. In addition to these councils the metropolitan holds a meeting of all his suffragan bishops every five years.

All these assemblies show a progressive tendency toward less frequent meetings and more curtailed activities. After the Holy See, individual bishops are gradually assuming the most authority and responsibility. Recently, however, a new kind of assembly has been coming to the fore: one that has no official standing, but that is concerned with discussing the various religious, political and social problems being faced by the faithful and giving advice on these subjects to the councils—advice that is accorded ever-increasing attention. This is especially true of the assemblies of the cardinals and archbishops of France, held several times a year; these are presided over by the senior French cardinal and organized by a permanent secretariat situated in Paris. A similar type meeting is held by the bishops of Germany at regular intervals at Fulda—an arrangement here of especial value, in that it allows effective collaboration between bishops widely separated from one another. In other countries, however (such as Belgium, Holland and Austria), this coordination is effected by one of the archbishops—sometimes the primate, who traditionally holds a dominant role. But in no case is there any question of an official organization. Anything of that kind is confined exclusively to the archbishops and bishops.

4 / Dioceses and Bishops

The bishop plays in the ecclesiastical system a role of supreme importance, surpassed only by that of the pope. Canon 329 expresses this with legal brevity and clarity: "Bishops are the successors of the apostles, and by divine appointment are placed over the churches that they rule with an ordinary authority under the power of the Roman Pontiff." Within the limits of his diocese the bishop has complete spiritual and temporal authority over the faithful, insofar as they are members of the Church.

It has not always been so. In the early days of the Church bishops were considered successors of the apostles, charged as they had been with converting the heathen and with founding and directing churches. But lacking any centralized organization, and other bodies having grown up side by side with the episcopate, there developed in the course of the Middle Ages a series of fierce rivalries, which in the long run proved of great value, in that the need to bring them to an end produced a great degree of institutional efficiency. Just as the pope succeeded in establishing his primacy over patriarchs, metropolitans and bishops, so the bishops established their own superiority over the chapters of the cathedral and over other diocesan dignitaries. And so from all the confusion of the period there emerged a harmonious unity, expressed in that meticulously organized hierarchy which is the main pride of the Roman Catholic Church. This hierarchy represents a power that, established though it was in the Middle Ages, remains today one of the most important and unifying elements in the contemporary world. And in his diocese the bishop is the chief representative of that power.

The Nomination of Bishops

Until the fourteenth century bishops were chosen according to the electoral principle. Originally the electoral body was composed of neighboring bishops (often non-residential ones), the clergy of the cathedral, eminent ecclesiastics of the diocese (especially abbots), the citizens of the episcopal city, and representatives of the civil power. It was felt desirable that the bishop should be the choice of the whole body of the faithful—clergy and laity—as well as of those who possessed temporal power, since often the great officers of the kingdom or empire were chosen from the ranks of the episcopacy, and bishops often acted as the king's ministers in those lands that they held from him. After the tenth century laymen became all-important in the electoral body, and the practice of simony—the sale of ecclesiastical offices, which gave rise to other serious vices— became widespread. The upshot was the famous investiture controversy, the resolution of which put an end to lay domination of the appointment of bishops and insured that the electoral body would thenceforth consist entirely of clergy.

There next followed, in the course of the twelfth century, the second phase of this evolution: the formation of a fixed electoral college—the cathedral chapter—that excluded all prelates and other clergy. Even while this was taking place, however, signs of the phase after that began to appear, with the ever-increasing degree of intervention by the papacy. By using the right of appeal, by the principle of devolution, by mandate, and above all by reservation, the pope became by the fourteenth century the ordinary nominator of bishops. After that date this was accepted, and it remained only for canon law to affirm this right, to lay down the conditions of its exercise, and to make provisions for special cases.

The System Today. Today all bishops are nominated by the Sovereign Pontiff. In certain circumstances he can concede the privilege to an electoral college; however, this is only a concession, and may at any time be revoked. It applies to about twenty bishoprics in Switzerland (Basel,

St. Gallen, Chur), Germany (Olmütz, Salzburg) and elsewhere.

The rights of intervention of the civil government are usually laid down in treaties or concordats. In France, for instance, the President of the Republic confirms the nomination of bishops in Alsace-Lorraine, an area where no division was effected between Church and State when this took effect in the rest of France. But in most cases the rights of the civil power do not go this far, but consist either of drawing up a list of candidates that is submitted to the pope and from which a single candidate is chosen, or in the exercise of a right of censure that allows them to refuse for political reasons the appointment of a candidate nominated by the pope. All these concessions are under the control of the Congregation of Extraordinary Ecclesiastical Affairs and of the Secretary of State.

Promotions to bishoprics are prepared by the Consistorial Congregation, which follows a fixed pattern of action. The simplest form consists in addressing to the bishops and other ecclesiastical dignitaries of the country concerned a request for a list of candidates most suitable for receiving this honor. In England, Holland, Ireland and Australia, when a see becomes vacant the bishops of the country nominate three candidates from whom the Congregation makes its choice. In the United States, Canada, Scotland, Brazil, Mexico and Poland, the bishops of each province draw up at regular intervals a secret list of potential nominees for bishoprics. Although this practice has not received the official sanction of the Holy See, it seems to be the one most common in Catholic countries.

Whatever the technique adopted, however, the same stipulations apply to all candidates. They must be priests, of legitimate birth, at least thirty years old, of high moral standards and intellectual distinction (possessing at least a licentiate in canon law or theology), and outstanding for their piety and administrative ability. Only the Holy See—by means of secret inquiry—may judge a candidate's aptitude.

Canonical Induction. The choice of a candidate is only the first step in the nomination of a bishop. It is followed by the canonical induction—the official concession of the office, which can be promulgated only by the pope. This is proclaimed in consistory and disseminated by the dispatch of three letters, one addressed to the nominated candidate, one to the chapter, clergy and faithful of the diocese, and one to the metropolitan of the province. Between the time he is nominated and the time he receives his letter of appointment, the candidate is known as a "nominated bishop"; once canonically invested he is a "bishop elect," until the moment of his consecration. Once he has been nominated he must make an act of faith before a representative of the Holy See, and swear two oaths: one against Modernism, the other of loyalty to the Holy See. Consecration takes place within three months following his investiture, and confers the order of the episcopate upon the candidate, giving him the plenitude of ecclesiastical powers and above all the right to administer all the sacraments. Consecration usually takes place in the metropolitan cathedral of the province in which the newly appointed bishop is living at the time of his elevation, and is usually presided over by the archbishop. Within four months of his canonical investiture, and after being consecrated, the new bishop must visit his new see and present his apostolic letter of appointment to the chapter in the presence of the chancellor of the diocese. Thenceforth he possesses all the powers of a bishop in residence.

Capitular Vicars.   Sometimes a bishop may be unable to exercise jurisdiction within his diocese, either for physical reasons (such as exile, imprisonment or insanity), or because he has been prevented by the spiritual sanction of excommunication. In this case, unless the Holy See has taken steps to find a substitute, or until it does so, the direction of the affairs of the diocese are in the hands of a vicar-general, who is nominated by the bishop himself if he is capable of so doing, or if not, by the cathedral chapter.

When a bishop dies the chapter elects within eight days an ecclesiastic who fulfills all the duties of the bishop during the vacancy of the see; he has the title "Vicar Capitular." The chapter also nominates an administrator, who has charge of the temporal affairs of the diocese during the vacancy. Thus, the chapter, on the death of a bishop, becomes the depository of the episcopal jurisdiction, which it delegates to the Vicar Capitular. If it cannot reach a decision about whom to nominate, the metropolitan has the power to do so. And, in special cases, the pope can appoint an Apostolic Administrator, who oversees the diocese until a new bishop is appointed.

The Functions and Powers of a Bishop

The cross, the ring and the miter are the symbols of a bishop's power, and he has the right to wear a violet soutane and a violet cord on his hat. The power represented by these symbols can be exercised by the bishop only within the limits of his own diocese, and not outside it or in any place declared exempt in respect of privileges received from the Holy See. They are "ordinary" powers—inherent by divine right in the episcopal office, and direct, i.e., immediately exercisable over any lay or clerical member of the diocese. The episcopal function therefore cannot be considered a delegation of the powers of the pope, and bishops are in no way "prefects" of the Holy See.

His Duties. Every bishop is bound to reside in his own diocese under the control of his metropolitan, and he may leave it only for a maximum of three months each year and then only for serious reasons. On the other hand, the bishop is bound to visit all the parishes of his diocese regularly, and they and all other ecclesiastical establishments under his control must be inspected by him personally at least once every five years. He can, however, nominate a vicar-general to carry out the visitation of places other than parishes. Such a visitation consists in meeting the people of the parish, visiting the churches attached to it, and checking the details of the temporal administration.

Every five years—in France, in years ending with a 2 or a 7—the bishops of a country must submit to the pope a report on the religious activity of their dioceses. This is done when they make the visit *ad limina* (to the threshold), which they must undertake every five years; in the course of it they make a pilgrimage to the tomb of St. Peter, and are received by the Holy Father.

Finally, every Sunday, and on a large number of religious feast days, the bishop must celebrate a mass for the faithful. This is known as the *missa pro populo*—mass for the people.

His Powers. Insofar as his duties are concerned, the bishop enjoys two kinds of power: those of order and those of government. The first kind, which is markedly religious and spiritual, is implicit in his episcopal office; it involves the administration of the sacraments. In his own diocese the bishop administers the sacraments of confirmation and ordination. He can also excommunicate people, induct abbots, receive the vows of nuns, consecrate elected bishops and crown kings. To these characteristic episcopal functions must be added the power of celebrating pontifical mass and vespers, consecrating chalices, altars and churches, blessing bells and cemeteries, and similar rites.

In his capacity as a governing administrator, the bishop rules both the spiritualities and the temporalities of his diocese. He is the direct and effective head of all the diocesan clergy, whom he controls, nominates and can defrock. His authority is limited by canon law and the decisions of the Sovereign Pontiff and the Roman Curia. Nevertheless a considerable degree of latitude is allowed him in interpretation and application, as well as in all matters regarding the discipline of the clergy (what vestments may be worn, whether or not clergy may attend theatrical performances and similar functions, and so on). These powers also apply to priests from another diocese who happen to be residing in his.

The bishop is also the supreme authority for all spiritual matters in his diocese. He alone has the power to give absolution in specially grave cases, and he is the supreme arbiter of all spiritual disputes that he may summon before him. Nevertheless he usually delegates these powers. He has also to watch over the spiritual welfare of the faithful, via episcopal letters, preaching and the establishment of schools. These schools are of three kinds: major and minor seminaries, specially charged with the education of future priests; secondary schools, run by the secular clergy under the direct control of the bishop; and primary schools, administered by the parish clergy.[1] In the same way, either directly or through delegated powers, the bishop presides over the religiously oriented activities of laymen.

[1] In certain dioceses there are also universities or institutes—centers of higher education. These draw their pupils from several dioceses but depend on the ordinary of the diocese in which they are located.

Finally, the bishop administers the property and revenue of the diocese; for this purpose he employs a specialized staff. Each diocese has its own revenue, which goes directly to the bishop and is known as the episcopal *manse*. The bishop also receives a percentage of the charges levied by the clergy for religious services, such as marriages, baptisms and funerals.

The Bishop's Assistants

Auxiliary Bishops.   In certain specially important dioceses the bishop needs the assistance of capable and efficient assistants who can, if necessary, replace him. In the early Middle Ages this function was performed by archdeacons, but their role began to diminish in importance at the beginning of the twelfth century. In our own time, all large dioceses, and those where the bishop—a cardinal or metropolitan—has numerous other duties to perform, have coadjutors. These are appointed under the same conditions as are candidates to the episcopacy. The term "coadjutor" is applied to those who automatically take over the succession to the see on the death of its present holder; they are often attached to a bishop who is ill, or who for any other reason cannot fill his office. Those coadjutors who do not have the right of succession are known simply as "auxiliaries." Both types possess full episcopal powers, which they exercise through a delegation of authority. They are titularies of those dioceses that, being situated in non-

Catholic countries, have neither clergy nor laity; in such cases they are known as bishops *in partibus infidelium.* They are actually titular bishops. Among them we must also include papal nuncios (who also receive the episcopal dignity) and other prelates on whom the pope may confer the title for honorary reasons.

The Diocesan Curia. The bishop has the assistance not only of his coadjutor but also of the diocesan curia. This includes all those organizations that participate in running the diocese from day to day—the episcopal council, the secretariat, the consultative theological committee, and above all, the Administrative Council, comprising lawyers and barristers whom the bishop chooses himself; these look after the property and revenue of the diocese. The curia is, strictly speaking, composed of the administrative and judicial organs of the diocese.

The judicial organs are the court of original jurisdiction for all cases between members of the clergy (since canon law forbids priests recourse to a lay court) and for all purely religious matters, except those reserved for the pope. An appeal can be made from a diocesan tribunal to the superior jurisdiction of the metropolitan, and thence to the Holy See. The makeup of the bishop's court is the same as that of the metropolitan. Both are presided over by an official who hands down the decision in the name of the bishop; he is assisted by a vice-president and various other officials, an auditor, a notary, bailiffs and so on. These officials are all nominated by the bishop, to whom they swear an oath of loyalty and obedience. They are bound to keep secret all matters coming within their knowledge. The bishop also has the power to summon before him all cases he thinks may involve some matter of particular delicacy.

Of the diocesan administrators the most important is the *vicar-general,* the origins of whose office are the subject of much controversy among historians.[2] In our time the vicar-general is an official nominated by the bishop, if he has need of him, who exercises in the diocese the powers of a bishop, without, however, having received episcopal orders. The only stipulation is that for certain matters the vicar-general must have a precise mandate from the bishop. In the diocesan hierarchy the vicar-general takes precedence immediately after the bishop, and before all other dignitaries.

The other members of the curia are the chancellor (sometimes assisted by the vice-chancellor) and the ecclesiastical notaries. Their function is to draw up the bishop's pronouncements and decisions, to register and classify them in the diocesan archives, and to maintain the other archives (often of great antiquity) that certain

[2] Some see in the vicar-general an official who has come to replace the archdeacon, who in the Middle Ages was the bishop's auxiliary but who in the course of the eleventh century became too powerful and was replaced by an official with a strictly judicial function. Others believe that the vicar-general was originally concerned mainly with matters of litigation. Yet another opinion is that his office originated from the need for substitute-bishops to fill in for those away for long periods on the Crusades.

churches still possess. All are "official witnesses"—that is, their signature on a document guarantees its authenticity in the eyes of the Church.

In addition to the services provided by the curia, the bishop can also rely on the help of the *diocesan synod,* which he is obliged to convoke at least once every ten years. This comprises the main officials of the diocese as well as certain parish priests; the bishop promulgates its decisions as vested with his own authority. At each synod synodal examiners are appointed who help the bishop in the disposal of benefices for a period of ten years. To their number are added certain parish priests who act as arbitrators in the event of conflicts (such as the refusal of a priest to accept his removal to another parish).

The Chapters. For a long time the function of episcopal synod was performed by chapters comprising all the ecclesiastics who collaborated with the bishop; we have already touched upon their function in the election of a bishop. The word "chapter" was also applied to all bodies of priests, monks, canons and the like who assembled at regular intervals to perform the Divine Office in choir. There was therefore a distinction between cathedral chapters and collegiate chapters—either regular (if they observed a religious rule) or secular (if they were ordinary priests); and this gave the name "collegiate" to the churches in which these latter functioned. The members of both kinds of chapter were known as *canons.*

Actually chapters are bodies that participate in the

administration of the diocese and the cathedral; they possess revenues (*mensa canonica*) that go to the canons, or "prebends." The pope alone can create or suppress chapters, but with the exception of those chapters expressly excluded from the jurisdiction of the ordinary of the diocese, it is the bishop's right to nominate "titular canons," as they are called. These dignitaries have a right to a stall in the cathedral choir and a vote in capitular assemblies. They are bound to live near the cathedral and to celebrate together certain parts of the Divine Office. On the death of a bishop it is they who nominate the vicar-capitular and the administrator of the diocesan possessions. They are under the authority of one of their number whom they elect; he is known as the Dean, and is usually assisted by a secretary. Strict regulations govern their daily lives.

Certain canons receive from the Holy See specific offices that they exercise under the authority of the bishop. Thus certain chapters have a canon-theologian who teaches theology on certain days fixed by the bishop; a canon-penitentiary who gives absolution in certain cases reserved for the bishop; and a parochial vicar who acts as parish priest for the faithful who come within the limits of the cathedral. Generally, however, the clergy who serve the parish of the cathedral are under the direct authority of the bishop, like all other parish clergy, and are not subject to the chapter as such. In all dioceses there are honorary canons. These have the right to wear the insignia of canons —the rochet, mozzetta, cape and ring—but have no special office to perform. Theirs are simple honorific dignities, like those the pope bestows on specially meritorious clergy when he makes them *monsignori*, prelates of his own household, or apostolic prothonotaries. Finally, in those cathedral churches that do not have a chapter, the bishop appoints at least four diocesan consultors, who are reappointed every three years. Their function is to make decisions about important matters when the see is vacant.

Such, then, are the various organs of the diocese, functioning under the overall authority of the archbishop or bishop. In mission countries, and lands that the Holy See has not yet divided up into dioceses—which it only does when it thinks fit—the missionaries are grouped together in vast territorial units directed by Vicars Apostolic and Prefects Apostolic. The former, named by papal brief, are usually vested with episcopal powers, though with only limited power to confer orders. The latter, nominated by decrees of the Congregation for Propaganda, do not have episcopal powers, but in a general way exercise a jurisdiction similar to that exercised by the Vicars Apostolic. Both are therefore delegates of papal power, and they hold mandates from the pope. Only the Vicars must perform the visit *ad limina,* but both types of official have to send a report to Rome every five years; and each year they must remit statistics regarding the number of baptisms, conversions and so on. They must also hold regular meetings of all the missionaries in their area, and oversee the recruitment and organization of local clergy (who, when they have become sufficiently numerous, eventually form the framework of the diocesan organizations that are set up. The vicars are assisted by a provicar, whom they nominate themselves.

It is thus obvious that these shock troops of Catholic propaganda depend far more closely on the General Headquarters of the Church than do those other religious soldiers who are established in countries "conquered" long since. The organization of these we must now analyze.

5 / The Parish and Its Clergy

Since medieval times the diocese has been subdivided into a number of districts to facilitate both the bishop's control over his clergy and easier administration. As we have seen, the bishop's main collaborators were at first the archdeacons, the successors of those auxiliary-bishops who were concerned with the religious life of remote and rural districts and who had no fixed place of residence. The archdeacon also exercised those powers that have since devolved on the vicar-general and other officials. Today each diocese is divided territorially into several districts, directed by ecclesiastics to whom canon law gives the name "Rural Deans." Each district comprises several parishes.

The Main Subdivisions of the Diocese

The Principal Districts. The ecclesiastic at the head of one of the districts into which the diocese is subdivided is nominated by the bishop and can be replaced by him. He is chosen from those parish priests possessing high personal qualities or administrative abilities. He must reside either in his own district or in a neighboring one; he takes precedence over the other clergy, and has a seal of his own and the right to participate in diocesan synods. To facilitate his performance of these duties, the bishop usually chooses the parish priest of one of the larger churches.

But no fixed rules determine the different divisions of the diocese; this is entirely the responsibility of the bishop. Certain dioceses are first of all divided into archdeaconates, headed by an archdeacon—usually the vicar-general—who controls the religious and administrative affairs of the clergy and makes regular visitations.

Most dioceses are also divided into deaneries controlled by a dean who is usually the priest of the largest parish in the deanery. Whereas the role of the archdeacon is mainly an administrative one, that of the dean is more limited and more clearly defined. While it is rare for deaneries to be presided over by officials of the former category, the latter are quite numerous.

Functions. Rural deans are merely the delegates of the bishop for certain matters that either he, the provincial council or the diocesan synod expressly specify. No ecclesiastical status distinguishes them from ordinary priests, and their function consists merely of control and supervision—for both of which they need a superabundance of tact. Their authority does not extend to the laity. They must insure that the clergy in their district preach zealously to the faithful, teach the catechism to children, comfort the sick and live permanently in their parish, observing the rules laid down by the bishop. Rural deans are especially concerned with the material state of the churches, liturgical vessels, statues, and in general, all the property belonging to the parish. They visit all the clergy of their district regularly, and make sure that when they are absent through illness or any other cause, a proper substitute is found.

In practice, it is generally the archdeacon who is immediately responsible for these different tasks, the deans being mostly concerned with classifying and forwarding the necessary information to the higher authorities. Moreover, in each deanery—or whatever the relevant ecclesiastical district is called—there are held, on dates fixed by the bishop, meetings of all the clergy in the component parishes; these are known as *ecclesiastical conferences.* Presided over by the dean, they are concerned with the main religious activities of the area and with examining or deciding about various administrative measures. They are at the same time occasions for spiritual and doctrinal instruction; and all the priests of the district must participate in them unless they have a very serious reason for not doing so.

Once a year the deans send the bishop a report on the religious activities of their deaneries, laying special stress on those matters requiring immediate decision—especially relative to the upkeep of the Church—and pointing out any scandals or abuses. On such matters they are advised to act with great prudence and the strictest discretion, lest by overemphasizing their personal judgment they should in any way hurt the reputation and susceptibilities of any other member of the clergy. (When there is a question of public scandal they are called upon to distinguish clearly between those matters for which they have actual material evidence and those based merely on rumor or hearsay.)

Such is the general pattern of activity and responsibility of rural deans. Vital though it is, it remains largely unknown to the laity, who only see those clergy with whom they come into daily contact: the parish priests and their representatives.

Parish Priests and Their Parishes

History and Definition. The first parishes in the West appeared between the fifth and seventh centuries. Originally they were centers of religious life outside the boundaries of towns, with their government in the hands of the bishop's auxiliaries. Gradually, however, there began to appear resident local clergy who lived in the *villa* or manor and ministered to the religious needs of its inhabitants. Then, with the increase in population and the tendency for conglomerations of people to cluster around centers of population (such as an abbey or castle) there came an inevitable tendency for natural divisions of the diocese to arise. Each village came to have its own church and to become a parish. During this period the choice of the parish priest was in the hands of the local magnate, who, having in many cases provided the church itself, felt he had a right to designate its incumbent. From the beginning of the eleventh century, however, first the papacy, then the local bishops, began to resist this practice (which had inevitably led to serious abuses). Eventually the participation of the laity in such matters became limited to the control of certain temporal matters of the parish. Today, although generally every village has its own parish, larger towns have several, according to the size of their population. Canon law distinguishes two kinds of parish: those in which the incumbent cannot be removed without his consent (except, of course, for moral turpitude); and those in which he can. All new parishes belong to the former category.

The parish is under the control of the parish priest or rector, and there can only be one to a parish. According to Canon 451, "The parish priest is the 'moral person' [i.e., the spiritual entity] to whom the parish has been confided, and his is the responsibility of looking after the care of the souls in the parish [hence the words "cure" or "curate"] under the direction of the ordinary." These "moral persons," who are considered as rectors of a parish, are usually chapters, monasteries and religious establishments that delegate their authority to a priest known as a "vicar"; he has the same powers as the original delegator. In mission countries the vicariates and apostolic prefectures are divided into units that may be regarded as the equivalents of parishes. Each has at its head a priest with powers analogous to those of a parish priest.

Finally, the function of a parish priest is permanent and stable, and although not of divine origin it is not a delegation of episcopal power, for the bishop cannot remove a parish priest from his office except for very grave reasons. Nevertheless under the authority of the dean the parish priest is subject to the bishop who nominates him.

Nomination. With the exception of parishes that belong to a "moral person," and apart from certain fairly rare cases (laid down in papal decisions), every parish receives its parish priest as the result of a nomination by the ordinary of the diocese. The procedure varies slightly according to the political regime under which the clergy of the country live; in certain cases the lay powers have the right to propose a candidate or to confirm the bishop's choice. But in all cases only the bishop can give an incumbent the right to exercise the powers of his office in the religious and ecclesiastical fields. A vicar nominated by a "moral person" has to be presented to him, and to receive from him the spiritual jurisdiction of his parish.

Canon law demands that a candidate for the office of parish priest have been ordained, and that he be outstanding for his sanctity, intelligence and fervor. He must also have done well in the examinations that every young priest must pass in the course of his first three years—and in some dioceses even longer—out of the seminary. When a parish becomes vacant the bishop, with the help of the synodal examiners, holds an inquiry on these points, and nominates the new priest within six months of the occurrence of the vacancy. If the new incumbent has had a previous parish, all that is necessary is to inform him of the change and to obtain his consent. However, if he has never been a parish priest, he must undergo an examination in doctrinal matters before the synodal examiners. In certain countries the practice persists of applying the canons of the Council of Trent (reaffirmed by a bull of Benedict XIV in 1742), according to which vacancies to parishes are filled by competition, either special, if for a specific parish, or general, if to provide a list of candidates worthy of becoming parish priests.

The Duties of a Parish Priest. As soon as he is nominated a parish priest can exercise his jurisdiction in his parish, in which he is installed with solemnity. But before this takes place he must make a profession of faith before the bishop, and take an oath against Modernism. Once installed, he must reside within his parish, which he cannot leave without a good reason—holidays being accepted as such—and without informing the ordinary. He must carry out his religious duties—saying mass, administering the sacraments, visiting the sick and poor, teaching the catechism—for the spiritual needs of the faithful, for whose benefit he offers up, on certain days fixed by the bishop, a *missa pro populo*.

His Function. On the whole the powers of a parish priest are "ordinary"—derived directly from his office. He cannot be replaced except for very grave reasons, but his powers can be delegated to someone else. He is the immediate head of all the religious activities of the parish, and no other ecclesiastic can exercise any jurisdiction or perform any office within the parish without his express permission, with the exception of the Sovereign Pontiff, the bishop or anybody they may appoint, since in both cases they exercise an immediate and direct jurisdiction.[1] Certain of these powers are directly spiritual, while others are administrative; but none of them are legal or judicial. A parish priest cannot promulgate edicts or make decisions in legal cases. All he can do in such matters is to advise, warn and admonish.

The parish priest's duties are first of all to regularly

[1] This is in fact the reason for the originality of the Catholic Church's organization. No bishop can exercise jurisdiction within his diocese without having received his powers from the pope, but once he has received them their ordinary use cannot be in any way restrained without very good reason. In the same way, a parish priest receives his powers from the bishop, but they are not a mere delegation of powers.

celebrate the Divine Office in the parish church, and to administer the sacraments. He must also teach the faithful regularly by his sermons, instruct children in the catechism, comfort the sick (giving Extreme Unction when death is imminent) and so on. There are also certain tasks that only he, or a priest specially nominated by him, can perform: the administration of solemn baptism, the publication of ordinations, banns of marriage and the performance of the ceremony, officiating at funerals, the carrying of the Blessed Sacrament to the ill, the blessing of the font on Holy Saturday and of certain houses when the occasion arises, and the right of hearing confessions and of giving absolution in those cases that he cannot delegate to another. The exercise of this religious activity is rounded off by the obligation to keep up to date the four main parish records containing information about all the faithful of the parish— the registers of baptisms, confirmations, marriages and deaths—in connection with all of which he has to issue the necessary certificates, authenticated with the parish seal. Finally, in certain parishes he has to maintain the daybook of the parish; this gives complete information about all parish activities. He is generally responsible for the parochial archives.

The parish priest is also the administrator of the parochial revenues. These include those that insure his own livelihood, comprising the fees he can levy for the celebration of mass. (Canon law specifies, however, that he cannot exceed the sum fixed in each diocese for such serv

ices, and part of it in any case goes directly to the bishop.)
To this must be added the sums that, like any other priest,
he can ask for various religious services, and a portion of
such religious dues as the tithe. He is also the administrator
of the funds provided by various means for the benefit of
different parochial organizations and for parish good works.
He can delegate these responsibilities to members of the
parish. But he is not, in a general sense, the *administrator*
of the church or of its material possessions, this responsibility being laid on the shoulders of the bishop, who nominates a council composed mostly of laymen to undertake
everything connected with such matters. Nevertheless the
parish priest has a considerable say in the disposal of all
funds raised by subscription for the decoration and maintenance of the church. All these different duties demand
great adaptability in the person responsible for them.[2]
When the parish is large, several curates assist the parish
priest to discharge his duties.

Curates. This word is used to describe those priests
who have the permanent duty of participating in the ministry of a parish under the direction of the vicar or parish
priest. They are nominated directly by the bishop, who,
however, must consult the parish priest before making a
public announcement about their appointment. In those
parishes that belong to religious orders the curates are

---

[2] When, owing to lack of priests, there is no incumbent for a
parish, the duties are undertaken by the vicar of another parish, a
process known as "holding a plurality."

presented to the bishop, who gives them their canonical induction. Curates are usually young priests who have just emerged from the diocesan seminary, where they have completed five or six years of study subsequent to an ordinary secondary school education. They have been taught theology, canon law and scripture, and initiated into the practical side of the ministry. After having received the tonsure, the seminarian receives the minor orders—those of porter, lecturer, exorcist and acolyte—then the major orders of the subdeaconate, the deaconate and the priesthood. He then leaves the seminary, and except in a few cases where he may be called upon to take up teaching or similar activity, is sent out to a parish.

The powers the curate exercises are merely delegated to him by the bishop or parish priest, and a priest who has not been endowed with such powers may not participate in any kind of parochial activity nor administer the sacraments, except in the case of imminent death. Once installed, however, the curate carries out, in the name of the parish priest, all the administrative or religious functions proper to him, and receives from the bishop the right to hear confessions and give absolution. The parish priest must assure him a reasonable standard of living, including accommodations, food and pocket money (his own mass-offerings being taken into account in this respect). He has to furnish the bishop an annual report on these matters. The duties of a curate come to an end when he is moved to another parish or is promoted to the post of parish priest.

To complete this picture of the lower secular clergy, we should note that there are certain priests who take over the duties of a parish priest when for any reason he is incapable of performing them; others who assume these duties when the parish priest is away from his parish for more than a week; and yet others who are appointed to direct the administration of a parish when there is no parish priest. There are also priests who do not form part of the parochial system—chaplains, almoners and teachers. They are under the jurisdiction of the diocese in which they live (with the exception of army chaplains, who have a special organization of their own, usually headed by a bishop).

Every member of the secular clergy is either attached to a diocese or directly subject to the Holy See. This "incardination" (as it is known in canon law) applies to every cleric from the moment he receives the tonsure. Only if we know this can we appreciate the breadth of the Catholic structure and the detail of its construction. The office of priesthood that a cleric receives on the day of his ordination can only be exercised by the power of the bishop, and within certain geographical limits fixed by that power. It is impossible for an outsider to comprehend the degree to which a cleric's spiritual enrichment, external rights and duties, and contacts with other Catholics are rigorously controlled by the place he occupies in the ecclesiastical hierarchy. The degree of freedom and rights of the regular clergy vary according to the different ideals of the institutions to which they belong, and the privileges the Holy

See has granted those institutions. But their personal activities are determined entirely by the organization to which they belong, and an analysis now of the main characteristics of these institutions will perhaps throw further light on the organization of the Church.

6 / The Regular Clergy

In addition to its minutely organized secular hierarchy, the Catholic Church has at its disposal a large number of religious bodies, all oriented toward its service. Together these bodies are known as the *regular clergy*, because instead of living in the world their members lead a community life according to a rule, or *regula*.

Their General Organization

Definitions. Canon 487 of the *Corpus juris canonici* (Corpus of Canon Law) defines "the religious life as a staple form of existence maintained in a community in which members of the faithful undertake to observe in addition to the common laws of the Church the evangelical precepts of poverty, chastity and obedience." Thus anyone who makes a public declaration of these three vows, which may be solemn or simple, permanent or temporary (if the latter, they must be renewed throughout life) is known as a religious.[1] In addition to these three obligatory vows, each religious institution may, according to its own principles, demand other and similar undertakings.

There are a great number of such religious institutions —either for men or women—whose rules have been approved by the ecclesiastical authorities. Those that contain a large number of members who take solemn vows are known as "orders." A "monastic congregation" is a grouping of various monasteries under the authority of one abbot, while a "religious congregation" (known more simply as a "congregation") is an institute whose members, known as "religious" or "sisters," take only simple vows. Women who take solemn vows are known as "nuns." Finally, canon law describes as "religious societies" those associations whose members live in common under the authority of a superior, following rules approved by the religious authorities but not taking the three ordinary solemn vows. Such, for instance, are the Oratorians, the White Fathers and the Sisters of Charity.

General Administration. Those religious orders de-

[1] By "public" is meant before an authorized religious superior representing the Church, and within the framework of a religious organization whose members in virtue of these vows live a community life and which has received the appropriate ecclesiastical sanction.

scribed as "of papal right" receive from the Holy See a decree of approbation; whereas those of "diocesan right" receive this decree from the ordinary of the diocese. But since a bishop can approve the existence only of religious congregations, monastic congregations and religious orders as such are dependent for their existence on the pope. And no bishop can authorize the existence of a new foundation until he has consulted the Roman Congregation of Religious Orders, which serves as an intermediary between the Holy Father and all religious institutions. However, this congregation has seldom impeded the creation of numerous purely local congregations—especially of women—which exist side by side with the great orders and the monastic congregations (for each of which the pope appoints a Cardinal Protector to give help and advice). All the institutions, such as the great orders, that have received the right of exemption, are not subject to the jurisdiction of the ordinary, although some are exempt by virtue of their vow of obedience.

Internal Organization. The precise organization of every religious institution is fixed by its own rule, and its internal government varies in rigidity and in degree of centralization with the nature of its activities and the ideals it has established for itself. The great orders and the principal congregations are usually governed by powerful organizations, and are divided territorially into provinces (created by the Holy See) and houses. These are established whenever the occasion demands, and where the funds necessary for their support are available. Purely diocesan institutions cannot establish houses in other dioceses.

Above the superior of a house are to be found those whom canon law describes as "Major Superiors"—the Provincial and his representatives, the Abbot Primate or Abbot Superior (for monastic congregations), the Abbot (for autonomous monasteries), and the Superior-General for religious orders of other kinds. The powers they exercise over the religious under their control are laid down in rules and regulations that allow for a wide variety of organizations, ranging from the most authoritarian to the most permissive. But every institution must hold at fixed intervals a chapter, an assembly that deals with problems concerning the order as a whole.

Superiors are subject to certain obligations. They must reside in a house of the order, must publish every five years a report about the activities of the order, and must pay regular visitations to all institutions under their control. (The bishop of a diocese must visit all non-exempt houses every five years.) With the help of their assistants the superiors look after the temporal goods of the order (which, since individual members are bound by the vow of poverty, must be vested in the corporate body). The revenues of an order derive from the lands it possesses, certain commercial activities and the numerous gifts made by the faithful.

Before a religious can become a Major Superior, certain conditions must be fulfilled. He must be born of a legitimate or legitimatized marriage; must be over thirty (forty to be a Superior-General); and must have taken his religious vows at least ten years before his appointment. All such superiors are elected, the system of election varying according to the rules or practice of the order.

The institutions of the Church also lay down certain general rules that must be observed before one can become a religious. All nuns bound by perpetual vows and all lay brothers (clerics who are mainly occupied with manual work, and who never become priests) must be postulants for at least six months. They must be unmarried Catholics who have already received the sacrament of baptism and confirmation; be at least fifteen years old; and in the case of certain orders of nuns, must bring a dowry to the convent. After being postulants for the prescribed period they must then become novices for at least a year, under the supervision of a master of novices. Then, if they so wish, they may take temporary vows, and as soon as they are twenty-one, solemn vows, of which a written record is signed and kept. In addition to this program, a large number of male religious can then become priests, following the pattern for secular priests.

Such is the body of canonical institutions that the Roman Church imposes on all religious orders. The specific characteristics of each depend on the special constitutions determining its activities. It is by the working of these different regulations, both specific and general, that the regular clergy participate in the communal activities of the Church.

The Role of the Regular Clergy in the Church

Classification. The various religious orders may be classified according to their manner of practicing the vow of poverty. Thus we can distinguish non-mendicant orders from mendicant ones; the latter can possess in common neither real estate nor goods capable of bringing in a fixed revenue, and like the Capuchins, they can own only what they need for their board and lodging. (The mendicant orders also include the Dominicans and the Augustinians, whose original rules forbade them to own land or property, but who have subsequently been relieved of this restriction by the Holy See.)

Another important distinction is that between the contemplative and the active orders. The former spend most of their time in contemplation and the recital of the Divine Office, although a hundred small details distinguish them from each other; in this category are found the Benedictines, Cistercians and Carthusians. The latter, such as the nursing orders, indulge in some form of activity. And halfway between are those mixed orders that combine both lay and ecclesiastical activities—such as the Jesuits, Dominicans, Franciscans, Carmelites and Premonstratensians.

Religious orders are also classified according to the

type of constitution that governs them. Some have their own special rules—such as the Carthusians and the Jesuits —while some base their rules on one or another of the four great ancient rules of St. Basil, St. Benedict, St. Augustine and St. Francis of Assisi.

The General Activity of the Religious Orders. A study of history, especially medieval history, affords us some idea of the part played by the religious orders in the life of the Catholic Church. We discover first the existence of monastic institutions that offered the select a material and spiritual framework within which their internal life could reach those ideals of Christian perfection after which they strove, while simultaneously giving them an opportunity to participate by means of their riches, example and general power in the positive and creative life of the Church. Typical of these monastic institutions were the Benedictines, the Cluniacs and the Cistercians. Since such orders were considered contemplative ones, their prayers and mortifications were regarded as intercessions before God for the whole of the Church.

Then there began to appear those orders, increasingly numerous as time went on (and including Franciscans, Dominicans and latterly Jesuits), that were dedicated to exercising a direct effect upon society through charity, teaching and preaching. Most of these were outside the structure of the episcopal hierarchy and depended directly on the Holy See, so that their role was quite important. They formed a militia under the direct command of the pope, and their work was universal. Indeed, the papacy came to look upon them as the best instruments for effecting its decisions, for unlike the local clergy they were not confined by the framework of a regimented hierarchy with its national limitations and sense of independence, and their activities could be conducted on any front. Nor were they hampered by the constant obligations of running parishes and other parochial chores. Today these orders' major activities are in four areas: preaching, education, "Catholic action" (the application of the principles of Catholicism to social and political life), various good works in the fields of medicine and philanthropy, and missions, in which the White Fathers, Jesuits, Oblates of Mary Immaculate, and other orders participate. Thus, in forming these various orders into groups, the Holy See has put itself in a position to use them where it sees fit to complement the daily work of the secular clergy.

And so we end our study of the practical institutions and hierarchy of the Roman Catholic clergy. We cannot but admire the perfection of its organization, the meticulous detail of its administrative system, and the majesty of its overall structure. The hierarchy is the outcome of nearly twenty centuries of history, the result of constant experiments based on a continuous willingness to profit from the lessons of history. It has made the Catholic Church one of the most imposing organisms in the contemporary world, secure in its foundations, difficult to upset or disorganize, quick to react to any challenge. At the same time, however, it is an organization that sometimes seems a little hide-bound, and we may well criticize its conservatism, immobility and slowness to adapt to change. But it must be remembered that the Church's very size naturally retards the speed of its reactions, and that if it were to attempt to find a more supple, rapid and independent system, it would not only run the danger of destroying its hierarchy and impairing its dogma, but would lay itself open to losing that essential unity—achieved through the omnipotence of the pope—that is a key point of Catholic belief.

Moreover, as we study the institutions of other religions we come to realize how difficult it is to achieve a real synthesis. Instead of an evenly divided pyramid, we find structures of many different kinds, varying from country to country, locality to locality, liturgy to liturgy. This is especially so with Protestant institutions, and these we shall now examine.

Part Two
THE PROTESTANT CHURCHES

7 / The Geography of Protestantism

Despite the extreme diversity of the various Protestant groups, we can detect certain organizational patterns, certain general characteristics shared by the different sects. But since in every land there are several different forms of Protestantism, each controlled by its own rules, we must first have recourse to a historical sketch and a geographical table.

The Genesis of Protestantism

The Reformation. In the course of the sixteenth century the reaction against the scandals and abuses that had become apparent in the Roman Catholic Church led to a series of secessions therefrom. In certain cases the "reformers" and their disciples laid down both their own con-

89

ception of Christian dogma and the form of the organization they wished their new religion to follow; this was true of the Lutherans and the Calvinists, for instance. In other cases (for instance, the Anglicans) these first Protestants were concerned not so much with formulating a new type of doctrine as with merely rejecting the authority of the Holy See; and they did not bother to set up an alternative form of organization.

The history of the Reformation became more and more complicated. Spreading in every country anxious to throw off the yoke of Catholicism, the new movement had to mold its beliefs and organization according to its contexts; this was true both of thought and morality (affinities with Lutheran and Calvinistic thought) and politics (support or hostility of the state). Moreover, within each original grouping a diversity of tendencies soon made themselves apparent, determined by whether or not it was necessary to create and define new dogmas, disciplines and organizations, and also by the extent to which the rejection of the all-powerful authority of Rome had provided scope for a hitherto unknown freedom of action. Finally, the colonization of the Americas, mostly by Europeans from the older countries of the West, accentuated still further this diversity. If on the one hand South America, populated by colonists of Spanish and Portuguese descent, remained Catholic, North America on the other absorbed people of every Christian persuasion and every sect that had grown up or suffered persecution in Europe. These achieved in the New World, thanks to the different conditions of life prevailing there, a spectacular success, which allowed them to proselytize other countries and even to bring new blood and a more ardent faith to those of their coreligionists who had remained in the Old World.

The Diversity of Protestant Institutions. Thus there emerged a multiplicity of groupings, sects and churches. Those founded by Luther or his disciples came to be known as Lutheran or Evangelical; their dogma is founded on the Apostles' Creed, the Nicene Creed and the Athanasian Creed, the Confession of Augsburg, the Articles of Smalkalde, the two catechisms of Luther, and the Book of Concord. But even apart from the sharp differences that separate their doctrines, liturgies and disciplines, these Lutheran groups present no real unity. In the same way, even if internally the so-called Reformed Churches (which are of Calvinistic origin), seem to present a certain unity in their common use of a synodal organization, there are also to be found beside them entirely independent sects, with completely different institutions. Too, certain countries have "established churches"—churches united to the state and directed and controlled by it. (This union or its reverse is determined by whether or not the government opposed or embraced the early movements toward church reform.) All these considerations throw light on the great geographical and historical diversity of Protestantism.

The Geographical Distribution of Protestants

Europe. A religious map of Great Britain, one of the centers of Protestantism, presents a complex picture. Side by side with the Roman Catholics, who number 4.5 million (besides 2.7 million in Eire) are the Protestants, divided into a great number of churches, of which the most important is the Anglican, or Church of England. The established church, it consists at least theoretically of some 20 million adherents. (Of course, many of these, though of Anglican descent, no longer practice their religion.) A recent estimate puts the number of practicing Anglicans of all ages at 6.5 million. The Established Church of Scotland, which is completely different from the Anglican Church, has 1,315,466 adherents. There are also members of this church—known as Presbyterians—in Ireland (136,-432), England (70,000), and various other Commonwealth countries, for a total of about 300,000. Other important religious groupings include the following:

Baptists 324,181	Quakers 80,000
Methodists 1,086,426	Seventh-Day
Congregationalists 244,761	Adventists 8,681

There are also varieties of Lutheran sects, the Church of Ireland, the Free Churches and many other bodies.

On the Continent only the Scandinavian countries have Lutheran Churches; these include most of the population and are established by law. The Danish Church numbers

4,002,700 out of a total 1962 population of 4,581,000; that of Norway, more than 2,800,000 (90 per cent of the total population); and that of Sweden 6,300,000 (95 per cent of the total); while in Finland the established Lutheran Church embraces 98 per cent of the population. Such unity and unanimity are exceptional, however, and the only country outside Scandinavia that presents a remotely similar picture is Holland, where the population is divided between the Dutch Reformed Church, Calvinistic and synodal, and virtually—though not officially—an established church (50 per cent); the Roman Catholic Church (35 per cent); and a variety of Lutheran, Mennonite, Evangelical and other sects (8 per cent).

All the large Protestant countries on the Continent evince the same diversity as Britain. In Germany the figures are as follows: Lutherans, 54 per cent; Roman Catholics, 31 per cent; Reformed Churches and Presbyterians, 5 per cent; Baptists, Methodists and others, 0.6 per cent. Among the Lutherans, however, we must distinguish various sects divided from one another by institutional or doctrinal differences. The same holds true in Switzerland, where more than half the population is classified as Reformed Church or Presbyterian (the other Protestant sects only adding up to some twenty thousand persons) although there is a great diversity of sects and churches. In fact, not only are there differences of dogma and discipline, but each canton tends to adopt its own ecclesiastical policy, according to the particular religious needs of its inhabitants. When, for instance, the federal government has decided to be separate from any specific religion, one often finds one or several established churches. (At Neuchâtel in the canton of Geneva, which has decreed a division between church and state, there are, for instance, three.) However, in the ten cantons where Catholicism is the majority religion, the Protestants can only organize non-established churches, though in some cases these are affiliated to the church of a Reformed canton. From this we can deduce something of the religious complexity of Switzerland.

In Catholic countries we seldom find the Protestants quite so subdivided, since in such cases unity better serves their purposes. In France, for instance, where there are slightly more than a million Protestants, the Reformed Churches and the Presbyterians number 735,000, divided into various groups; the Lutherans, 235,000. However, a great measure of unity has been achieved within the framework of the Reformed Church of France, which embraces a majority of the churches and sects. In Alsace-Lorraine the organization of the Protestant churches is different from the rest of France, because the law dividing church and state did not come into operation there.

The situation in Czechoslovakia is similar. There are Reformed and Evangelical churches—that is, Calvinist and Lutheran—but there is a larger proportion of independent sects (25 per cent of all Protestants, who together make up a sixth of the population). In Hungary, the Presbyterian and Reformed Churches—the most numerous—comprise 20 per cent of the total population, though there are also important groups of Lutherans (6 per cent). In Rumania there are 75,000 members of the Reformed Church, 400,000 Lutherans and 150,000 Independents; together they are a minority in contrast with the 13,000,000 members of the Orthodox Church. Finally, we should note the numerous Protestants in the U.S.S.R. (2,500,000, of whom 350,000 are Baptists) and Poland (1,000,000, of whom 835,000 are Lutherans); and the very few to be found in Italy, Spain, Ireland and Greece.

The United States and Elsewhere. We can easily understand the complexity of Protestant beliefs and organizations if we examine the religious situation in the United States. A 1960 statistical analysis of the adult members of each church gave the following figures:

Baptists	19,934,467
Methodists	11,945,786
Lutherans	7,400,999
Presbyterians	3,963,387
Anglicans	2,852,965
Disciples of Christ	1,922,484
Congregationalists	2,179,394
United Church of Christ	2,170,214
Mormons	1,437,652
Roman Catholics	37,563,851
Jewish	5,200,000
Greek Orthodox	2,595,266

Source: *The Annual Yearbook of Churches.*

The Baptists are divided into eighteen sects arranged in nine different groupings; the Methodists, into nineteen sects in four groupings: the Lutherans, into twenty-two sects in eight groupings; and the Presbyterians, into nine sects. The federal census of 1936 listed 256 denominations (sects and churches), and though this does not necessarily imply the same number of institutional rules, it at least indicates an impressive number of them. The only characteristic common to all is their exemption from all property and personal taxation.

In Canada there is an even greater variety. Twenty Protestant groups represent 55 per cent of the population. The most important are the United Church (20 per cent), Anglicans (15 per cent), Presbyterians (7 per cent), Baptists (4.5 per cent) and Lutherans (4 per cent). There is no established church. In Australia the Anglicans (45 per cent of the population) are most numerous, but we must not neglect the Presbyterians (12 per cent), Methodists (11.5 per cent) and the various other sects (5 per cent). The same proportions and variety hold good in New Zealand.

Finally, all the other countries of the world are regarded by Protestants as mission countries, and so each reproduces the characteristics of the proselytizing country. This is especially so of such highly developed countries as the Republic of South Africa, where, side by side with the Anglican Church, flourish Lutheran, Methodist and Calvinist sects, whose numbers almost equal those of their counterparts in the United States. There has, however, been a growing trend toward unification.

Nevertheless the overall fragmentation of Protestant sects is great—all the more so in that we have grouped under several genuine types a large number of bodies united on voluntary grounds or for practical reasons, and in fact not possessing any total identity of views.

To undertake a study of the internal structural organization of all these groups would be impossible, for each itself contains groups with very different types of organization. The German Lutherans, for instance, have rejected the episcopal system, while the Scandinavian churches, which have exactly the same beliefs, have retained it, and divided their churches into bishoprics and archbishoprics. In the same way, although some Methodist churches have bishops, others do not, and have gone far in suppressing the hierarchical system and its authority.

Therefore, with the exception of certain churches that have been transplanted from one country to another (for instance, the Anglican, Dutch and Scottish Presbyterian Churches), and that for this reason have—apart from the fact that they are "disestablished"—retained the institutions of their mother church, there is only one fruitful approach: to concentrate entirely on the institutional side, and neglect the doctrinal. To do so is to acknowledge the major pressures of history. Some reformers merely refused to recognize the authority of the Holy See, but kept both the ecclesiastical hierarchy and a large part of the Roman ritual. Others —when the Catholic clergy of their country would not acquiesce—replaced the old system with a hierarchy of elected councils composed of both ministers and the faithful. And still others organized their churches on a local basis, completely independent of one another and united into a voluntary association merely by a vague set of beliefs.

8 / Protestant Organizations

Three main kinds of Protestant church organization may be found concurrently in all countries. However, except in the United States, it is usual for one to predominate.

Episcopal Organizations

The episcopal system has been kept by the Church of England and by all those Anglican churches that Englishmen took abroad with them. It is also the system used by the Methodist Churches and by the churches of Scandinavia.

The Church of England. When the English Catholic Church, instigated by the royal government, broke with the authority of Rome in the sixteenth century, it was not considered necessary to entirely transform its then existing rules. Therefore it remained organized into two provinces, Canterbury and York, the first commanding thirty dioceses, the second, thirteen. The two provincial archbishops are thus heads of the Church of England, but at the same time subject to the authority of the king; they have, moreover, the right to sit in the House of Lords, as do twenty-one bishops. The archbishops preside over all high ecclesiastical assemblies, and their courts of justice are the courts of appeal above the diocesan tribunals. The Archbishop of Canterbury has supreme jurisdiction in certain matters. As a last resort it is always possible to appeal from the provincial tribunals to the highest lay court—the Privy Council.

It would not be true to say that the two archbishops alone control the Church of England. Apart from frequent intervention from the laity, the assemblies actively participate in their government. "Convocations" gather regularly in each province; these issue canons, which are made obligatory upon congregations and clergy by royal sanction. The Convocation consists of two chambers: the High Chamber (diocesan bishops) and the Lower Chamber, in which are included the deans of the cathedral chapters and of the colleges of Westminster and Windsor, the provost of Eton, the two oldest archdeacons of each diocese, and members representing the lower clergy, at least three from each bishopric elected by the titular clergymen in each benefice and by certain other people, since every priest is eligible.

There are other assemblies where representatives of the entire Church of England meet, apart from the provincial organization. The Church Assembly, formed in 1920, meets at least once a year and is presided over by one of the archbishops. Its decisions apply to all the Church, but it does not rule on doctrine and theology; these cannot be modified without the consent of Parliament. The Church Assembly consists of three chambers: the bishops (from the High Chambers of both Convocations); the clergy (from both Lower Chambers); and the laity (members of congregations who are elected for five years). At the same time, since the Church of England is the proprietor of its churches, bishops' palaces and presbyteries, an Ecclesiastical Commission regulates the income of bishoprics and chapters, and provides the capital for salaries, retreats and prelates' and dignitaries' pensions. Finally, roughly every ten years, all the Anglican bishops both of England and from abroad meet at the largest assembly of all. These Lambeth Conferences—so called because they meet at the Palace of Lambeth, belonging to the Archbishop of Canterbury—are veritable Ecumenical Councils of Anglicanism. However, although they are very important they only allow for an interchange of views, and do not form part of the official structure of the Church of England.

Through its archbishops and various organizations the Church of England is closely linked with the state. Its real head is the Sovereign, who ratifies its main decisions and nominates the archbishops and bishops (whose jurisdiction is analogous to that of the Catholic episcopacy).[1]

The bishop, too, is aided by assemblies in which the faithful are represented. The diocesan synods that brought together all the clergy of the diocese have virtually disappeared, their place being taken by diocesan conferences that since 1919 have sat once a year under the presidency of the bishop. These have competence over all the administrative affairs of the diocese, and consist of a chamber of the clergy and one of the faithful, the latter consisting of the members of the Church Assembly and others either nominated by the bishop or elected by the laity.

In the same way each of the two archbishops is assisted by a Vicar-General of the province—always a layman—who controls the administration of the province through delegated powers. In each diocese there is also a lay Vicar-General; he cannot be removed from power, and he fulfills the same function, besides presiding over the bishop's court. The bishop also has an ecclesiastical assistant; in the more important dioceses this is a suffragan bishop, whom he can

[1] The traditional procedure for the appointment of bishops is as follows. The Sovereign sends a *congé d'élire*—a right to elect—and at the same time a letter indicating the candidate he has chosen (although actually the nomination is made by the Prime Minister), whom the chapter must elect. However, there has often been a tendency for chapters to revolt against this practice—so much so that the present system is tending toward the creation of an electoral body, composed of clergy and laymen, that would propose three candidates to the Sovereign.

appoint at will, and who corresponds to the Catholic Vicar-General. In others he is assisted by archdeacons who preside over subdivisions of the diocese that in turn are divided into deaneries and parishes. The parish is in the charge of a vicar whose nomination is in the hands of a patron—a landed proprietor, the chapter of a cathedral, a university or the Crown—that presents its candidate to the bishop, who accepts and installs him after he has sworn a number of oaths of loyalty to the Crown, the bishop and so on. However, certain trusts and foundations have been set up in recent times to buy the right of presenting livings from lay owners.

In the parish the vicar is assisted by an assembly of his parishioners known as the *Vestry* that assists in the running of the parish; by churchwardens, who are concerned with fund-raising and matters of ritual; and above all, by the Church Council, which consists of the vicar, the churchwardens, those of the laity who have been elected to the Church Assembly and other conferences, and other parishioners of both sexes. The Church Council is concerned with the temporal administration of the parish—buildings, budget and so on—and with the church ornaments and furniture, of which it is the legal proprietor. The vicar must heed the advice of the Church Council. He chooses his own curates, from young priests who must have a university degree or a diploma from a training college and who must have spent at least eighteen months in an Anglican theological institution. The vicar is thus in this respect much more independent of his ecclesiastical superiors than is his Catholic colleague, though at the same time he depends a great deal more on his parishioners. He has on the whole a much easier life than they, for his income is assured, and if he is married there are special increments to it. (Most of this revenue is derived from tithes, legal taxes on landowners— though these have greatly diminished in recent years—and from another sources, which are amalgamated into a fund known as Queen Anne's Bounty.)

Anglican churches outside England follow a similar pattern, the main difference being that since they are not established churches, the supreme authority is organized differently. Bishops are everywhere elected by chapters or by electoral assemblies. The Anglican Church of Wales, for instance, which was disestablished by laws passed in 1914 and 1920, comprises one archbishop and six bishops. The archbishop, whose seat is at Saint-Asaph, directs its affairs with the help of a legislative council (composed of prelates, clergy and laity) that requires a two-thirds majority to give its decisions statutory force. The situation is similar in Ireland, where two archbishops and eleven bishops are assisted by a Representative Body and a General Synod; in Scotland, with seven bishops; in Canada, with four provinces and twenty-four bishops, all directed by a primate elected by the assembly of bishops; in Australia, where twenty-two bishoprics divided into four provinces are directed by an elected President; in India, where there are fourteen sees; and in the United States, where the Church is known as the Protestant Episcopal Church.[2]

The Methodist Churches. In the course of the eighteenth century the Anglican Church went through a period of lethargy, until John Wesley (1703–1791) started a movement to inspire it with greater fervor. This was the origin of the Methodist Church, whose members, numerous enough in the United Kingdom, went on to establish in the United States branches that today are flourishing greatly. Most of them have retained the episcopal form of organization, their territories being divided into circuits headed by a superintendent. The laity have a greater voice in the running of affairs than in the Anglican Church, and are allowed to preach (although the administration of sacraments is reserved for ministers). This pattern is followed by the Wesleyan Methodists in England and by the Episcopal Methodist Church of the United States, in which the bishops, under the superintendents who preside over the districts, direct both priests and deacons.[3] Every year a

[2] We must also note the existence of a number of religious societies peculiar to Anglicanism; fifty-eight of them are for women, ten for men. Although their members sometimes take vows, these organizations have only sketchy structures. Also, there is the order of deaconesses, which helps the clergy mainly with problems connected with the female members of the Church. Deaconesses are also found in other Protestant churches, some of which have women ministers.

[3] The Methodist Episcopal Church South, the Colored Methodist Episcopal Church—which is quite large—and the African Methodist Episcopal Church are organized similarly. In addition to these,

conference is held to supervise all religious activity and to elect the dignitaries and prelates. Every four years a General Conference of ministers and laity takes decisions about matters of major importance and acts as a supreme court of justice. "Lay electoral assemblies" assign to members of the laity those functions not specially reserved for ministers, and nominate delegates to other conferences.

Lutheran Episcopal Churches. The established churches of the Scandinavian countries have episcopal institutions. In Denmark there are nine dioceses controlled by Parliament under the administrative direction of the Minister for Ecclesiastical Affairs. Side by side with the bishops, and at each stage of the church hierarchy, ecclesiastical councils make decisions about major issues and intervene in the nomination of bishops, although theoretically this is left to the state. The Norwegian Church consists of eight dioceses under the leadership of the Bishop of Oslo. The upkeep of the churches and the support of the ministers are assured by the state and the municipal authorities under the control of the Minister of Church and Educational Affairs. Parliament is the legislative authority and the high court of justice in ecclesiastical matters. The organization of the church in Sweden is somewhat similar.

Certain non-established Lutheran churches have also

----

moreover, there are also non-episcopal Methodist sects. Some 15 million Americans belong to episcopalian churches of one kind or another—Methodist, Anglican, Lutheran and others.

retained the episcopal system. This is true in certain parts of Central Europe. In Germany, where the churches are seeking a new form of organization, the principal body since 1945 has been the Evangelical Church, which is divided into twenty-five regions. The episcopal system also prevails in the United States, where the Lutherans are known under such names as Evangelical Church, Evangelical United Brethren Church and so on. On the whole, however, the tendency has been for the Lutheran Church, in those countries where it is not established, to adopt a non-episcopalian system of government.

Synodal Organizations

The two principal characteristics of those churches called "synodal" or "presbyterian," and usually of Calvinistic complexion, are the predominance of various kinds of councils, and the application of a democratic regime that, in giving a predominant role to the laity, sets itself against the monarchical system of the Roman Church.

The Reformed Church of France. This affords the most clearly defined example of the synodal type of organization. Formed in 1907 by the amalgamation of the Evangelical Reformed Churches, the Reformed Churches, the Free Evangelical Church, the Methodist Church and the Reformed Church of France, it is a loosely knit organization of parishes united by common adherence to the Declaration of Faith. It involves, therefore, not only a voluntary union, but also the acceptance of a hierarchy corresponding to a broadly defined doctrine.

The base of this hierarchy is the parish, at the head of which is the minister, its nominal shepherd, who is appointed for an unlimited period. He is entrusted with the direction of the spiritual affairs of the parishioners—with holding services, preaching, education and such matters touching the internal administration of the church as the keeping of the parish registers. He is bound by the disciplinary code of the Reformed Church of France and by the decisions of its synods. He cannot follow any other profession. To exercise his pastoral ministry he must have been registered by the Reformed Church of France; this registration is issued to those ministers who have not received it before by a National Commission of the Pastoral Ministry. Ministers must also have either exercised the ministry in some other church, or been ordained by order of the National Synod at a ceremony at which at least seven other ministers must take part. Strict conditions are laid down for a candidate for ordination. He must be a member of the Reformed Church of France, and of French nationality; at least twenty-five years old; have passed the final examinations of a secondary school; and be a bachelor of theology. He must also have satisfied the requirements demanded of postulants for the ministry, and accepted the statutes and disciplinary code of the Church.

Candidates for a pastoral ministry submit their names to those parishes that are vacant. The Presbyterial Council of the parish is alone responsible for electing the titular pastor of the parish and all his assistants, although he himself can choose—and has to pay—his personal aides. All pastors receive a fixed stipend, drawn from the various revenues accruing to the whole church, the payment of which is obligatory on the entire body of the faithful. The apportionment of these funds is decided by local ecclesiastical bodies.

The real direction of the parish belongs not so much to the minister as to the Presbyterial Council, which is composed of the minister and at least five lay members. These are elected by secret balloting in which all the members of the parish over the age of twenty-five take part. The Council is elected for a six-year period; half the members retire at three-year intervals, those who retire being re-eligible for election. It is presided over by a minister assisted by at least a vice-president, an archivist-secretary and a treasurer, all of whom are elected by the laity. It must hold meetings at least four times a year, and if possible, once a month.

The local churches are grouped into territorial groups known as "consistorials." These are directed by an assembly, the "consistory," made up of all the pastors of the district and a number of laymen elected by the Presbyterial Councils; laymen must equal ministers in number. Elections take place every third year. The consistory's function is to direct and coordinate local activities while collaborating with the Regional Council.

The next higher division is into regions. These are controlled by fifteen regional synods. The regional synod comprises all the pastors of the area and an equal number of laymen, elected every third year, under the same conditions as those applicable to members of the consistory. Since it is not in permanent session it elects at its first meeting from its own members, by secret ballot, an executive council known as the Regional Council; this comprises from eight to twenty people, pastors and laymen being represented equally. This council, which appoints its own administrative staff, is together with the Synod the directing authority of the region. Its real function is to see that the decisions of the National Synod are carried into effect, as also those of the Regional Synod, which it itself convokes. The Regional Council is also responsible for watching over the spiritual welfare of all the different churches within its area.

At the head of the religious hierarchy is the National Synod. It meets every year, and is composed of deputies elected by the regional synods in proportion to the number of pastors each contains. It also includes representatives of the various theological faculties recognized by the Reformed Church of France, and is presided over by a moderator (chosen by election) who must be a pastor. He is assisted by two vice-moderators—one a clergyman, the other a layman—and by four secretaries, two clerical and two lay. He is responsible for looking after "the general interests of the Church." These include accepting or rejecting local churches, defining the limits of regional and consistorial boundaries, directing the various training colleges for future pastors (and pastors' appointments), and organizing the different administrative commissions and the National Council.

This last-named is composed of twenty members—ten clerics and ten laymen—who are re-elected at three-year intervals by secret ballot and by an absolute majority. The Council elects its own president, who must not be the president of the National Synod or of a Regional Council. He is assisted by two vice-presidents, a secretary and a treasurer. The council's function is to execute the decisions of National Synods and to prepare agenda for them.[4]

The Reformed Church of France is characterized by the great degree of autonomy enjoyed by the different parishes. These are ruled as much by the faithful as by the ministers, and are divided into electoral units. This same principle holds true also in the temporal sphere, with each parish being responsible for its own finances and property (which are administered by a kind of cooperative associa-

[4] Certain organizations, such as the various theological colleges (which are administered by an Academic Council) depend directly on the National Synod of the Reformed Church of France. The Central Evangelical Society, however, the body responsible for proselytism, has a certain degree of administrative and financial independence.

tion, the activities of all being coordinated on a national scale by a Union).

The Synodal Churches of Europe. A somewhat similar system operates in the Church of Scotland. At the same time, however, since this church is an established one, and its nominal head is the English Sovereign, the nomination of ministers has long belonged to patrons. This largely explains the various disaffections this Church has experienced in the course of its history, and the various schisms that have given rise to free Presbyterian churches. Like the established church, these generally consist of ministers (whose titles vary from Deacon and Pastor to Bishop) and laymen. Their joint activities are coordinated in such higher synodal organizations as the Kirk Session, the Presbytery, the Provincial Synod and the General Assembly, each of which is presided over by a moderator elected by his colleagues.

The Reformed Church of Holland, which is not established although the royal family belongs to it, is organized on a synodal pattern. It is divided into ten provincial synods, each including more than three hundred parishes and divided into circuits. Control at each level of authority is vested in a council, and the whole church is directed by the Principal Synod.

Similar institutions are found in the Swiss cantonal churches—Geneva, Neuchâtel and so on—which are of Calvinist origin, as well as in the various groups of churches of Lutheran inspiration. This is true of a certain number of German churches grouped in the Evangelical Church in Germany, of certain free Evangelical churches in the same country, and of both the cantonal and non-established churches of Switzerland. The same type of organization is also favored by numerous Protestant sects in those countries where Catholicism predominates, in various areas proselytized by Calvinists, and in certain French churches of Calvinist or Lutheran origin (especially in Alsace-Lorraine, where those churches that were not subject to the Law of Separation do not form part of the Reformed Church of France). To this list must also be added those English Methodists who have adopted the presbyterian system in preference to the episcopal.

The Synodal Churches of America. Numerous synodal churches in America owe their origin either to the transplantation of groups from the Old World, or to the expansion of a European movement. Such are the Church of Scotland in Canada and the United States, the Presbyterian Church of the United States, the Presbyterian Church of Cumberland, the Presbyterian Church of North America, the Reformed Church of America, the Christian Reform, and among Lutheran sects, the Evangelical and Reformed Church, the Lutheran Evangelical Synod of Augsburg in America, and so on. But there also exist certain offshoots of churches that, although episcopal in their country of origin, on being transplanted to America were transformed into organizations in which the faithful assumed those powers of control that had formerly been exercised by the state. The most typical example of this procedure is furnished by the Norwegian Lutheran Church of America, founded in the New World by Scandinavian immigrants who belonged to the established church of Norway. This is one of the consequences of the spirit of absolute religious liberty that prevails in the United States, and is a tendency encouraged by the very nature of Protestantism, which from time to time has encouraged the growth of an even looser, more independent type of organization—congregationalism.

Congregational Organizations

Definition. Within this category must be included all those Protestant bodies not organized according to the episcopal or synodal system. The fundamental characteristic of these bodies is the autonomy of the local group within the framework of a free organization. Thus there is a voluntary association, without any acceptance of a special dogma or general doctrine. The purpose of such an organization is to facilitate religious life and worship, the basis of all such groups being the preaching of the Divine Word in its primitive purity, without constraint and free from any discipline or criticism other than that of the Holy Spirit as it illuminates the human soul. Those systems of authority that are set up are purely administrative—finance, building, ministers' salaries—or connected with religious propaganda (made easier by large organizations) and strictly practical objectives (such as teaching and the education of ministers). Collective descriptions such as "company" or "confraternity" would therefore be more suitable than union or congregation.

We may, however, distinguish between certain groups. On the one hand, there are large organizations that include many faithful, and possess precise and well developed organizations; on the other, more limited societies that include only a small number of local establishments, and that have no administrative system more elaborate than that of a pastor—specially chosen—who directs communal worship. Finally there are sects—the name might fittingly be applied to the whole congregational movement—that meet only to invoke the Holy Spirit and to pray to the Lord; they have neither pastor nor minister.[5]

Thus it is easy to understand how complex these congregational organizations are. But this does not mean they are entirely devoid of discipline. On the contrary, some churches—such as the Latter-Day Saints, more commonly called Mormons—impose on their members very strict spiritual discipline. It is therefore impossible to study the

[5] The first category often also includes local associations, the individual units of which should by rights belong to the second. As to those sects included in the second and third categories, they are often grouped in bodies that have absolutely no religious purpose, but are concerned with such practical matters as good works and finance.

movement in any detail, but only to analyze those congregational organizations that have a large number of sects.

Congregationalists. Several groups of this name have developed, especially in the Anglo-Saxon countries. The movement's origins go back to the seventeenth century, when there grew up side by side with the Anglican Church congregational communities that in 1832 were formally organized into the Congregational Union of England and Wales. Since 1919 the churches that constitute this Union have been divided into nine provinces directed by moderators whose function is to advise the faithful. The provinces meet in the Union, which is presided over by a moderator, who may be a cleric or a layman. In addition, each local group and province has its elected committees and its general assembly, which makes major decisions. These groups are mostly concerned with the coordination of temporal activities and the organization of the ministry, which in Britain and the Commonwealth must be composed of persons who have been trained in a college recognized by the Union and who have undergone a probationary period of three years and passed an examination under the aegis of the local Unions.

In the United States there are several congregational groups organized in similar fashion. Since 1913 most of them have been grouped in a National Council composed of their delegates. This is headed by a General Secretary who coordinates the activities of the whole organization, which he represents at meetings of other confessional organizations.

Autonomy, liberty and coordination are therefore the characteristics of these groups.

Baptists. At the beginning of the seventeenth century John Smith and Thomas Helwys, provoked by their disagreement with certain aspects of the doctrine and organization of the Anglican Church, started a movement of which the two principal groups today are the General Baptist Church and the Strict and Particular Baptist Church. Both spread rapidly, especially outside Great Britain; and under the leadership of William Carey they were the first to organize missions in the non-Christian countries of Africa, and in India, working through the Baptist Missionary Society. In 1891 John Clifford succeeded in uniting these two sections of the Baptist Church into the Baptist Union of Great Britain and Ireland—a purely voluntary organization to which, however, certain sects such as the Strict Baptist Churches and the Open Baptists do not belong.

According to Baptist principles, local groups are free to organize themselves exactly as they wish, and to draw up whatever rules they think will be best suited to their local needs. These groups are divided into regional groups —nine in England, one in Scotland, and one in Ireland— controlled by a Superintendent who acts as a coordinator; the Superintendents hold a monthly meeting for this purpose. There are rules governing the payment of ministers, who must have attended a Baptist college and who cannot stay for more than five years at the head of one group. Other ministers organize lay preaching and like matters.

Outside the United Kingdom there are Baptists in the Commonwealth, France, Italy, Spain, Russia, Germany, Austria, Rumania, Hungary, Bulgaria, the Scandinavian countries and the United States. In the last-named, four-teen national Baptist groups coordinate local associations, but are independent of one another. The most important such group is the Baptist Convention of the South, which is especially important in rural areas; it has coordinating bodies known as "boards." There is also the Baptist Convention of the North, which comprises thirty-seven different sects, each with a large degree of autonomy. And too, there are the Negro Baptists.

The major characteristic of American Baptism is there-fore the immense proliferation of sects, some of them with very few members: Regular Baptists, Primitive Baptists, Free Will Baptists, Seventh Day Baptists, Six Principle Baptists, Campbellites, Church of God, and so on. This is a natural consequence of the lack of a hard and fast organization—a characteristic shared in America by the various independent sects, which are also very numerous, and some of which are quite famous. Who has not heard of the Churches of Christ, the Adventists or the Quakers?

However, despite the different forms Protestantism has taken, the mere need to set up some kind of organiza-tion has provided a means of understanding the general pattern of the whole movement. The maintenance of the old hierarchical system, a democratically functioning federalism, autonomy and coordination, absolute independence: one or another of these types of organization will always characterize any Protestant sect. The pressures the modern world exerts on people and ideas have tended to form larger groups—and hence have produced an ideal of Protestant unity. Various national, doctrinal and functional organizations have begun to appear. And, too, there are signs of a new super-congregationalism aimed at uniting in free association all the differing systems of dogma and types of organization. And above all, there is the ideal of realizing complete Christian unity.

9 / The Protestant Quest for Unity

During the past forty years the most important single fact in the history of Protestantism, and indeed perhaps in that of Christianity, has been the tremendous effort made to unite and coordinate the different churches. Various organizations have already made their appearance; the most important of them, the World Council of Churches, was established in 1939.

Groupings

National Groupings. Since the end of the nineteenth century there has been a marked tendency for the various Protestant groups in a given country to form some kind of association, either because of political pressure or because of the need to undertake common action of some kind. In

France, for instance, there is a Council of the Protestant Federation in which all churches are represented; in the United States, a Federal Council of Churches, and even a National Conference of Christians and Jews (as also in Great Britain). In England the Federal Council of Churches, together with the various Anglican bodies, tends to unite all the different Protestant bodies. In general, these organizations do not possess any very definite corporate structure; their purpose is to permit the interchange of views. They are tending to be supplanted by local committees of the ecumenical movement.

Dogmatic Groupings. Side by side with this movement, and occasionally anticipating it, another has become apparent in recent years: the appearance of bodies that unite Protestants of the same confession, denomination or system of dogma. Among such organizations are the Lambeth Conferences (already mentioned); the General Council of the Alliance of the Reformed Churches (created by the Presbyterians in 1910); and the World Baptist Alliance (1905). Apart from these international groupings, other, national ones follow the dogmatic divisions in one country. The American Baptists, for instance, are united in three great federations.

The Search for Unity of Action. Protestants have above all tended to seek unity and coordination of action on those specific points where diffusion of effort might lead to failure. In this way charitable organizations, youth movements and religious confraternities have come into existence. Proselytism in pagan countries has been fruitful in promoting movements of association, and has brought together Protestants of all sects and nationalities. In the course of the nineteenth century the progress and success of Protestant missions were considerable. By 1923 there were 29,000 missionaries, 10,000 native pastors and an annual distribution of 10 million Bibles. Success was especially marked in Japan, Korea and those countries under Anglo-Saxon control.

These missions are directed by organizations, the first of which was founded in 1792 by the Baptist William Carey. In 1795 the Missionary Society of London, an interdenominational association representing most English sects, was founded. Others followed suit in England, the United States, Switzerland, Germany and France; and it naturally followed that churches appeared in those non-Christian countries that depended on these societies. In an inevitable tendency for these to form groups among themselves, new unions were formed. A growing desire for unification led the Americans in 1906 to call the first conference of Protestant missions operating in Islamic countries. This was followed by a second at Lucknow in 1911, and a third at Jerusalem in 1924. Meanwhile there had taken place the great missionary conference at Edinburgh in 1910, which had seen Protestant missionaries of every different kind of sect from all over the world come together. From that time on Protestant missions held definite and regular conferences in the International Council of Missions, a body whose interests now exceed those of merely missionary interest.

The World Council of Churches

History. In the course of the Edinburgh Conference, Bishop Brent of the Episcopal Church of the United States formulated a resolution calling on the churches to take seriously the prayer of Christ for his disciples "that they may be one." His action led to the formation in 1914 of the Universal Alliance for the International Unity of the Churches, which included the various Protestant sects of Europe and America, and eventually, the members of the Orthodox Church. After World War I, Brent and his colleagues resumed their activities, in the hope of bringing the different Christian churches together to resolve their differences about doctrine, and their various conceptions of the spiritual life. In 1927 at the Universal Conference of Lausanne was founded the movement known as "Faith and Order" (which, however, the Catholic Church refused to join). At the same time Archbishop Soederblom of Upsala was engaged in founding an association designed to transmit a message of peace to the world, and to solve the various problems besetting man. Stockholm in 1925 saw the answer: the formation of the movement "Life and Action."

After a series of discussions a congress representing the two movements was held at Oxford in 1937. A committee of fourteen delegates was formed, and their labors were crowned by the creation at Utrecht in 1939 of the World Council of Churches. Thenceforth non-Catholic Christianity was to have its own organization; its structure was formulated at Amsterdam in 1948.

Organization. Ecumenical institutions are founded on two principles. First, each church adhering to the organization must recognize the principle of autonomy—while admitting the interdependence of churches within one confession, it must not concern itself with the life and conduct of other members. Likewise the council must not be regarded as a legislative organ; it has no disciplinary or dogmatic powers, and is limited to overseeing the coordination of various activities and encouraging in every sphere the exchange of views likely to reinforce the spirit of unity. Secondly, the governing organs of the council are organized so as to represent both the main sects constituting the organization, and the main territorial divisions of the Christian world.

Any group of local churches prepared to respect these two principles may become a member of the World Council of Churches. To do so it must forward a request to the General Secretariat, which after making inquiries about the autonomy and stability of the prospective member, transmits its application to the Assembly. Not only are most Protestant sects (with the exception of those of Germany, which does not yet possess a comprehensive national union, and certain sects of the U.S.S.R. and the Soviet satellites) represented on the Council, but many Orthodox groups have also given their adherence. Up to this writing, however, the Roman Catholic Church has not done so.

Above the national committees that serve as intermediaries between the General Secretariat and the different churches are various interlocking organs, the frequency of whose meetings depends on their size. Only one of them sits in permanent session.

The largest body is the Assembly, whose meetings take place at intervals of several years. It is composed of fully accredited members (actually there is a maximum of 450) representing the various church-members, in the following proportions: 85 for the Orthodox churches of the world; 110 for the Protestant churches of Europe; 60 for those of Great Britain and Eire; 90 for the United States and Canada; 50 for Asia, Africa, South America and the Pacific islands; 25 for South Africa and Australia; and 30 for other groups. The desirable proportion of laymen has been fixed at one-third. Delegates may be of either sex; and they must represent the principal confessions of each region. (Others may participate in the Assembly without having voting powers, as for instance consultants sent by member-churches or by the Executive Council; observers accredited by churches not members of the Council; and delegates from youth movements and similar bodies.)

The Assembly discusses any question that may interest the World Council. At its first session it elects a president and appoints the various working committees. It also chooses the members of the nomination committee, who after consultation with the Executive Committee and the General Secretariat, put forward a list of candidates for the post of President of the World Council, which the Assembly fills by election.

But although it is the main body capable of taking important decisions, the practical authority of the Council springs from other bodies.

Among these is the Central Committee, which consists of ninety members elected by the Assembly on a proportionate basis similar to its own, and including at least twenty-one laymen. It meets at least once a year, and can be summoned at other times for exceptional reasons at the request of at least a third of its members or on the advice of the Executive Council. It elects its own president and vice-president, whose names are submitted by a nomination committee which it has appointed and on which the principal sects are represented. At each of its meetings the Central Committee supervises the execution of the various decisions arrived at by the Assembly, and answers specific problems submitted to it by the different churches. It votes the annual budget of the Council and is empowered to create all the offices the various ecumenical activities of the Council demand. The Committee gives an account of its work to the Assembly and itself nominates the Executive Council, on which its president, vice-president and twelve of its members have seats. The Executive Council meets twice a year to implement the decisions of the Central Committee.

The Assembly and the Central Committee together choose those permanent officials who are at the head of the World Council. These include first of all the Presidents elected by the Assembly, who automatically form part of the Central Committee and the Executive Committee. The six of them direct, control and coordinate all the activities of the movement; as a result they are the most influential people in it. On the other side there is the General Secretariat, with members appointed by the Central Committee, which forms the permanent executive organ, charged with the achievement of the ends proposed by the various assemblies, in liaison with the International Missionary Council. It includes a Secretary-General, Associate Secretary-Generals and a complete administrative staff; it is based at Geneva. (There are, too, other commissions—especially that concerned with finance, which has the responsibility of looking after the temporal wealth of the Council. It is supplied by subsidies contributed by the constituent churches.)

These, then, are the methods by which the non-Roman Catholic Christian world is endeavoring to achieve unity. Only the future will tell whether this task can be achieved, and whether beyond these early attempts there is possible hope for a complete union of all Christians. As matters stand today, the union only makes possible a certain unity of action and a fruitful interchange of views; it is essentially a "fraternity" based on common beliefs. But each church—and especially the Roman Catholic—maintains its own spirit and organization. To achieve complete unity by the creation of a new spirit and a discipline acceptable to all will involve the destruction of essential dogmas dear to innumerable Christians, and in the long run will involve the disappearance of that idea of moral and spiritual nonconformity that is still part of the heritage of a large section of mankind.

Part Three
JUDAISM AND THE
ORTHODOX CHURCH

10 / Judaism

In the modern world Judaism is essentially a racial concept, and despite the fact that the Zionist movement has concentrated a large number of its members in Israel, they are for the most part—though relatively few—widely dispersed. But Judaism is also a religion—one of the most ancient in the world—and as such has adherents in all countries.

The General Characteristics of Judaism

Its History. The origins of Judaism can be traced back to the very earliest times. The religion of nomads, its most original characteristic and one that appeared at quite an early stage was monotheism—the belief in one eternal God, Yahweh, the creator of the world and its inhabitants, who had "chosen" Israel from all the peoples of the earth to honor him and to keep his faith. This national religion was organized by Moses and his successors in a series of rigidly defined laws. There emerged a religious community, the *edah;* after the Babylonian captivity it became identified with the political community. The synagogue where the faithful met on feast days became the center of all communal activity. Over the centuries, despite numerous misfortunes and inevitable schisms, the Jewish people maintained both its existence and its practice of a religion that had been perfected by the Sages and the Prophets. At the same time, as the result of forced or voluntary migrations, Jewish communities came into existence throughout the eastern Mediterranean.

The destruction of the Second Temple by the Romans in 70 A.D. altered this position. Thenceforth Jews were regarded as "foreign subjects," but were permitted to form associations for the practice of their religion. At the same time they became dispersed through the whole Mediterranean basin, and so became established in Europe. The survival of these communities in the Middle Ages was made all the easier by the fact that the Catholic Church did not accord Jews the same rights as the rest of the population. The Jews were forced to live in restricted areas, forming corporations with their own laws, and depending on the protection of kings and feudal overlords. Their main occupation was commerce and moneylending, since usury— even when it involved only the smallest amounts of interest —was forbidden to Christians. This situation—often a hard one—lasted until the nineteenth century, when the growth of liberal ideas allowed the Jews to return with equal rights to the community.

The organization of Jewish communities did not present a uniform pattern. The fact that they were widely diffused, and the lack of unity and central authority resulting from this, the contact with different peoples and religions—all contributed to the breakup of the ancient system. The political and legal restrictions imposed on the Jews often forced them to modify their laws. In spite of this, the strength of a tradition unequaled among other races fostered the growth of organizations and institutions common to all the different groups, and reinforced by the Zionist movement's gathering of so many Jews in Palestine.

Its Ritual. The Jews of antiquity worshiped Yahweh in the Temple at Jerusalem, which was the center of Jewish religious life, synagogues being merely places where people collected for prayer (which is still true). The minister, who is called "rabbi," undertakes a highly specialized course of studies directed not only toward the understanding and teaching of Jewish thought and doctrine, but also toward a knowledge of the numerous regulations regarding fasts, feast days, and so on. The body of these rules, and the explanation of the various beliefs of the Jewish religion, are to be found in the Bible, which traces the history of the Jewish people and its expectation of the coming of the Messiah, and in various other sacred books, of which the most important is the Talmud.

Such are the basic elements that have molded Jewish institutions, the basic characteristic of which is formalism. In no other religion are the various acts of worship and religious behavior so strictly regimented as in Judaism. Observance of the Sabbath, ablutions, fasts, what foods may or may not be eaten—all are prescribed, with an extraordinary wealth of detail. (Indeed, one of the main activities of the rabbi is to answer the various problems connected with such matters submitted to him by the members of his congregation.) And although this ritualism may seem curious to those unaccustomed to it, we must remember that non-Christians are often equally puzzled by the liturgy of the Roman Catholics, the casuistry of certain reform movements, or the constant disputes about the sacraments that agitate other religions.

Judaism in Israel

Under the British mandate Palestine had 1½ million inhabitants, of whom 600,000 were Jews. Today the State of Israel (which territorially represents only a part of Palestine) contains nearly 900,000 Jews and some 250,000 Arabs and others. Nevertheless the religious organization is much the same as it has always been.

The Changes Brought by Independence. In the exercise of their mandate the British proclaimed complete freedom of worship, and did not subsidize any religion. The direction of Jewish affairs was confided to the Jewish Agency, the permanent representative of world Zionism. A Zionist Congress held every fourth year brought together Jews from all over the world, elected by their coreligionists, who nominated delegates for each country (especially Palestine); all of these together made up the Jewish Agency. The task of the Agency was to concern itself with all political affairs relating to Jewry, and especially with schools and problems of immigration and colonization connected with Palestine. For social and religious affairs, the Jews of these countries elected members to a special organization, the National Council, or *Vaad Loumi*, which, unlike the Agency, did not represent world Jewry. Rather, it was a kind of Palestinian Parliament, controlling religious matters, fixing rules for the election of the Chief Rabbi, and nominating other rabbis.

With the achievement of independence, the role of the Agency became limited to regulating the relationships between Palestine and world Jewry, and to questions of immigration. The National Council has been suppresed, and religious affairs now come under the direct control of the government. There is therefore an absolute union between church and state, made all the closer by the fact that religious laws often control civil life in such matters as marriage and the like, since the state laws for such matters have not yet been completely codified. The state therefore assumes responsibility for the support of rabbis and the maintenance of religious buildings, all matters concerning worship coming under the control of the Ministry of Religion, which is divided into five departments.

This situation has not escaped strong criticism. Among the immigrants to Palestine are many unbelievers—indeed, some three-quarters of the whole—most of whom accept with indifference the position of the rabbinate and the identification of the civil and religious calendars. (State holidays coincide with religious ones, in accordance with national traditions.) At the same time, however, there exist certain groups, especially in the new agricultural communities, that are positively antireligious, and opposed to the dominating position of the rabbis. The whole regime, therefore, is presently in a state of flux.

Israel's Religious Organization. The Jewish religion in Israel—*Kenesset Israel,* as it is officially called—is headed by the Chief Rabbi of Palestine, who is usually elected by the rabbis of the country and is under the direct control of the government. The Chief Rabbis of other countries— England, France and so on—as well as the leading personalities of world Jewry, also advise on the appointment.

The Chief Rabbi is assisted by the Grand Council of Rabbis, whose members are appointed by the state. With their assistance he directs and controls the activities of those Israelis who practice orthodox Judaism, and who are divided into communities at the head of which he appoints rabbis. But there are several groups that do not come within this framework. Some of these are directed by religious leaders who recognize the authority of the Chief Rabbi but are loosely autonomous within the general religious framework of Judaism. Such, for instance, are the Sephardim— Jews of Spanish origin who were expelled from the Peninsula in the fifteenth century and have since spread over North Africa, the Balkans, France, Italy and Great Britain, and of whom a certain number have migrated to Palestine. They are headed by a Chief Rabbi who is known as the *Richon Lesion,* "Leader of Zion." In a similar position are those Jews who come from Saudi Arabia, and whose leader, the *Hakham,* or "Wise Man," is subject to the authority of the Chief Rabbi. There are other groups who either recognize only the nominal authority of the Chief Rabbi, or else reject it altogether. The Hassidim, for instance, have an independent organization. The super-orthodox, or Kharedim, feel that the Chief Rabbi is not sufficiently strict in his religious observances, and they have their own rabbis.

The local unit at the base of the Jewish religious system is the *Kehilla,* or community. Each possesses one or several rabbis, who are nominated by the Chief Rabbi with the assistance of the Grand Council, and who are attached to a human group, rather than a synagogue. After finishing their studies, they must receive from the director of the religious academy at which they have been studying the power to hold religious services. This is done at a special ceremony known as the *Smikha-Lerrababnout.*

The authority of rabbis extends primarily to all strictly

religious matters, and to everything connected with ritual, the upkeep of the synagogue, prayers, religious meetings, the control of the young, authorized food (kosher), and so on. The rabbis may intervene in purely civil matters, such as marriage and the rights of succession. As the state has not set up a form of civil marriage, the only existing alternative in Palestine is religious marriage. In the same way only a rabbi can legalize divorces, which are very common in Israel because permitted by Judaism. Finally, when anyone dies intestate, the rights of inheritance are subject to religious laws of which the rabbi alone is the interpreter. The powers of the rabbis are therefore much wider than those of their Christian colleagues. But the union of church and state has serious drawbacks, of which the most obvious are the refusal of unbelievers to marry in synagogue and the difficulties created by marriages of Jews and Gentiles. Here again no definite set of rules governs the situation. Another source of confusion is that the stipend of rabbis is provided partly by the communities they serve, and partly by the government, which has taken the place of the old National Council of the Jewish Agency.

Judaism Outside Israel

Israel is the only country in which Judaism is the established religion, but there were in the world in 1960 an estimated 13,132,000 Jews. The most important groups were in the United States (6.2 million), the U.S.S.R. (3 million) and the United Kingdom (460,000, about half of them in London). No single organization brings them all together; their religious unity stems from adherence to authoritative written codes, the use of Hebrew for all ritualistic purposes, and constant emphasis on the study of talmudic and rabbinical texts.

Nor does there exist any hierarchical organization of the kind adopted by the Roman Catholic Church, for once he has been duly ordained each rabbi is the equal of any other. However, administrative necessity has resulted in the creation in most countries of some kind of governing body, and in the appointment of a Chief Rabbi. These bodies are partly synagogical, partly secular in composition. They are concerned not only with matters of discipline and the like, but with the regulation of the relations between Jews and the non-Jewish world. In the United Kingdom these functions are undertaken by the Board of Deputies (established in 1760); in the United States by the equivalent body in the Orthodox Jewish Congregation of America.[1] Closely related to these central bodies are the various agencies that supervise such religious matters as the licensing of ritually approved kosher butchers.

Yet although more united than the Christian churches, the Jews are not entirely undivided, and certain divisions

---

[1] The Chief Rabbi of the United Kingdom is also Chief Rabbi of the British Commonwealth, and as such exerts a considerable influence. This, of course, was even more the case when Palestine was a British-mandated territory.

have arisen among them in the course of their history. In the United Kingdom, for instance, besides the Chief Rabbi there is a Chief Rabbi of the Sephardic Congregation, which consists of the descendants of those Jews—the first to arrive in England when Oliver Cromwell relaxed the anti-Semitic laws in 1657—who came originally from Mediterranean countries, as opposed to their more numerous brethren from Germany, Central Europe and Russia. In contrast with this primarily ethnological division, there is also a doctrinal one, which tends to cut across world Jewry. With the breakdown of the ghetto and the growth of liberal and rationalistic ideas in the late eighteenth century (the term "orthodox" does not appear in a Jewish context until the time of Napoleon), the Reform movement started among European Jews. In 1810 the first Reform temple was opened by Israel Jacobson at Seesen, Germany; the movement later made great headway in the important port city of Hamburg. In the United Kingdom, Reform Judaism now centers on the Liberal Jewish synagogue; in the United States, on the Union of American Hebrew Congregations (founded in 1873), the Central Conference of American Rabbis (with about four hundred members), and the Jewish Institute of Religion (founded in 1922).

The development of Judaism has followed no single pattern in any one country, and a complete contrast with Britain and the United States is provided by France, where state intervention made itself felt in the growth of most religious institutions. The Jews obtained civil liberties by a

law of September 27, 1791, but the suppression of all civil
and religious corporations resulted in the complete dis-
organization of French Jewry. Not until the Napoleonic
decrees of 1806 and 1808 was French Jewry resurrected—
in a consistorial system maintained at the expense of the
faithful. In 1831 rabbis were put on the same footing as the
ministers of other religions. All previous regulations were
summed up in the ordinance of May 25, 1844, which remained the fundamental law regarding the Jewish religion
in France until the separation of church and state in 1905.
Since that date the dominant fact has been that the with-
drawal of state support has thrown the responsibility for
the organization of the Jewish religious community upon
itself.

Each locality containing a number of practicing Jews
has several synagogues, in each of which services are held
under the direction of a rabbi who has been trained at the
rabbinical school in Paris and chosen by the congregation
itself, subject to the approval of the Chief Rabbi and the
Central Consistory. These synagogues come under the control of sixty-three various associations within the framework
of nine consistorial regions—Paris, Bayonne, Bordeaux,
Besançon, Epinal, Lille, Lyons, Marseilles and Nancy. The
associations themselves are grouped in the Central Consistory—with headquarters in Paris—the supreme authority
in all religious matters. The Consistory is composed of the
Chief Rabbi of France, two other rabbis elected by their
colleagues, and fifty lay members representing other as-

sociations. The Chief Rabbi's authority extends over some forty other rabbis, but not over the fifteen or so "reformed rabbis" who acknowledge in him only a moral superiority.

In Alsace, where there is a large Jewish community, the laws of 1844 are still in force, and the various synagogues are grouped in consistories controlled by the Prefect of the Department and the Minister of Public Worship.

11 / The Orthodox Church

Distinct from and independent of the Catholic and Protestant churches of the West is another great Christian body that participates in their basic doctrinal beliefs, and is divided from them rather by historical and cultural factors than by dogma. Although the schism between East and West had been implicit in the division between the two sections of the Roman Empire, it did not become final till after the Council of Florence (1429). Whereas the West depended upon the traditions of Roman law, and derived from them an unrivaled administrative system, the East looked toward the traditions of Hellenistic philosophy, and showed more concern for doctrinal and metaphysical issues. The one emphasized humanism, the other theocracy. In the West, the hierarchy of power was immutable; in the East, even the slightest degree of ecclesiastical absolutism was suspect.

Organization

The Orthodox Church has been described as "an oligarchy of patriarchs," and its constitution, administrative patterns and relations with the temporal powers have largely been determined by historical rather than religious factors, and by the nature of its cultural context rather than by considerations of dogma or theological preoccupations.

Its constitutional development began in 1453, the year Byzantium—the city of Constantine—fell to the Turks. Before that date the determining factor had been the close alliance between the Church and the Basileuses—the eastern emperors. The immense influence of Constantine's administrative reforms extended to the churches of both East and West; in both, the secular unit of administration—the diocese—was duplicated exactly in the spiritual world. In the East the head of the ecclesiastical diocese was the Exarch, corresponding to the Western bishop; and each group of dioceses—usually smaller than their Roman counterparts—was loosely united under a metropolitan. The whole world (or as much of it as was apparent to the medieval mind) was divided into patriarchates. Rome and the whole of the West were considered one such, the others being originally Constantinople, Antioch, Jerusalem and Alexandria. Each patriarchate was considered an individual entity, although a certain preeminence attached to Rome and—to a lesser extent—Constantinople.

As the rift between East and West became more pronounced, the patriarchs of Antioch, Jerusalem and Alexandria came to lean very heavily on Constantinople (which, largely because of the East's greater preoccupation with theological speculation than with administrative efficiency, never achieved the kind of dominance exercised by Rome). Throughout the whole of its history the Orthodox Church has never possessed a unifying principle stronger than that which evolved from the personal characteristics of any one patriarch. Nor has there ever been any kind of federal assembly for the whole of eastern Christianity. But it should be pointed out that Orthodox theologians have always attributed to an ecumenical council a doctrinal infallibility similar to that which Roman Catholic dogma attributes to the pope.

The prestige that accrued to the so-called Ecumenical Patriarch derived until the fifteenth century largely from the fact that the seat of his authority coincided with that of the supreme secular authority. The Emperor himself was considered quasi-divine, and the Church, because it derived its authority and prestige from him, was largely dependent on the lay power and its administrative organs. Preoccupied with problems of doctrine and metaphysical speculation, the Patriarchs of Constantinople were busy deciding the validity of religious images; at the same time their Roman contemporaries were engaged in the investiture controversy, which was to result in the independence of the Church.

The inevitable consequence of this alliance between church and state was that when, in 1453, the Greek empire ended its long decline by falling to the Turks, the spiritual prestige of Constantinople declined noticeably.

The Rise of National Churches

The four patriarchates—which, since the time of Constantine, had depended on the Ecumenical Patriarch— were in no sense nationalistic. They derived their importance either from the fact that they had occupied important positions in the Roman administrative system, or as in the case of Jerusalem, because of the prestige they had acquired in the history of Christianity.

New factors now began to have effect. The Church became identified with the purely national outcome of the struggle with the Turks; the identification with the state, which in the case of Byzantium had resulted from the prestige of the Empire, now became the by-product of a bitter struggle for survival. Orthodox Christianity became identified with the nationalistic aspirations of its component parts; this process, as the recent history of Cyprus and the part played in it by Archbishop Makarios has shown, continues today. For four centuries a vast process of fragmentation occurred, similar in some ways to the rise of national churches in the West, but different in that no doctrinal factors were involved. The occasional charges of doctrinal incompetence hurled at Constantinople were intended to excuse rather than explain movements toward what was virtually administrative independence.

In 1589, Russia, which had been converted to Christianity by Byzantine missionaries, broke away and established its own church under the Patriarch of Moscow. Two centuries earlier, what is now Yugoslavia had achieved semi-independence under the Serbian Patriarch; and Cyprus, under the Archbishop of Constantia, had never quite fitted into the patriarchal system. The formal independence of the Greek Church, under the Archbishop of Athens, was established in 1833; that of Rumania, in 1864; and that of Bulgaria, in 1870, under the control of an exarch. The breakup of the Hapsburg Empire at the end of World War I resulted in the ecclesiastical independence of Albania (under the Archbishop of Durazzo). Other examples of the process of disintegration have been the setting up as independent churches of the provinces of Finland (1923) and Japan (1940); these had originally been dependent on Moscow, for the Russian Church was the only part of the Greek Orthodox body that had indulged in any extensive missionary activity. Mention must also be made of the independent enclave of Georgia under its Catholicos, and of

Sinai, which under its own Patriarch became in 1575 (and still remains) the smallest self-governing church in the world, with some 150 members.

Today the 30 million Orthodox Christians in the world[1] are divided among the four ancient patriarchates and their more recent fragmentations. The largest is that of Rumania (13,200,000), the smallest (apart from Sinai) that of Japan (45,000), which secured its independence from Moscow under the Archbishop of Tokyo as a result of World War II.

In all, there is a supreme Patriarch, an Archbishop, bishops or exarchs (who are unmarried and therefore chosen exclusively from the members of monastic establishments), archpriests or archimandrites, and priests, who may marry (though only once). The central organs of administration—less formal than those in the West—depend on the Patriarch, who is usually assisted by a permanent Holy Synod consisting of a fixed number of his dependent bishops, half of whom are re-elected annually, and a National Council—analogous to the Church Assembly of the Anglican Church and representative of the lay and political viewpoint. In all matters of church government the secular authorities have a greater influence than has ever been true of the Roman Church. All branches of the Orthodox Church have played a considerable part in the recent ecumenical movements.

---

[1] This figure does not include either the Russian Church, or those 2 million Christians who, although still following the ritual and practice of the Greek Church, remain in the Roman communion.

The Russian Church

With its 20 million members[2] the Russian Church occupies today—as indeed it always has—an important part in the affairs of Christianity. Once the control of Constantinople—whose missionaries first established Christianity in Russia—was shaken off, the Russian Church rapidly identified itself with national aspirations, and its representatives were instrumental in extending the Russian Empire and establishing the hegemony of Moscow. An important event in this marriage of church and state occurred in 1721 when Peter the Great abolished the Patriarchate of Moscow and vested supreme power in the Holy Synod, the most influential member of which was the Imperial Procurator.

The monasteries, which produced churchmen, statesmen, and that peculiar Russian phenomenon, the *startsy*, or spiritual guide,[3] were not only the backbone of the church, but also, as on the occasions of the Polish and French invasions, centers of national resistance.

Upon the outbreak of the Revolution in 1917, a council of all the Russian churches restored the Patriarchate of Moscow, and made a number of reforms. There then followed a lengthy period of proscription, during which the official policy of the government was to discourage all forms of Christianity. Curiously enough, this did not result in the

[2] *The Times,* November 19, 1961.
[3] The most notorious example of whom was Rasputin (1871–1916), the "spiritual guide" of the last Czarina of Russia, Alexandra.

Russian Church's becoming identified with anti-Communist elements; and when the German invasion came, both clergy and laity identified with the national struggle. Largely as a result of this, and partly because of the more liberal policies followed by Stalin's successors, the Russian Church is today fairly free from persecution and the more stringent forms of state control. There is a Patriarch in Moscow, metropolitans in other important cities, and in 1961 the Russian Church was admitted to membership in the World Council of Churches.

Bibliography

Yearbooks and Directories

The Baptist Handbook. London: Baptist Union. (Annual.)

The Catholic Directory. London: Burns. (Annual.)

The Congregational Year-Book. London: Congregational Union of England and Wales. (Annual.)

Crockford's Clerical Directory. Oxford: The University Press. (Annual; Church of England.)

The Jewish Year Book. London: "Jewish Chronicle." (Annual.)

The Official Year-Book of the National Assembly of the Church of England. London: Church Assembly and S.P.C.K. (Annual.)

The Scottish Episcopal Year Book and Directory. Edinburgh.

The Year Book of Jehovah's Witnesses. Brooklyn, New York.

The Ecumenical Movement

Anglicans and Methodists Talk Together. London: S.P.C.K., 1960.

Kraemar, Hendrik. *World Cultures and World Religions*. Philadelphia: Westminster Press, 1961.

Leeming, Bernard. *The Churches and the Church*. Westminster, Maryland: Newman Press, 1960.

Religious Orders

Canu, Jean. *The Religious Orders of Men*, tr. P. J. Hepburne-Scott. New York: Hawthorn Books, 1960.

Hoffer, Paul. *A Guide for Religious Administrators*. Milwaukee: Bruce Publishing Co., 1959.

Missions

A Decisive Plan for Christian Missions: The East Asia Christian Conference of 1959. London, 1960.

Martin, K. *Beginning at Edinburgh: A Jubilee Assessment of the World Missionary Conference of 1910*. London, 1961.

Judaism

Baron, Salo W. *A Social and Religious History of the Jews*. 2d ed. 8 vols. and Index. New York: Columbia University Press, 1960.

Bernstein, Philip S. *What the Jews Believe.* New York: Farrar, Straus and Cudahy, 1951.

Gronfield, I. *The Sabbath: A Guide to Understanding and Observance.* London, 1906.

General

Bailard, F. *An Introduction to Religious Sociology,* tr. M. J. Jackson. London, 1960.

Chancellor, F. B. *What's What, A Complete Guide to the Church of England.* London, 1960.

Corneils, J. *Oecumenical Annals of the Catholic Church: An Historical Outline.* Edinburgh, 1960.

Highet, J. *The Scottish Churches: A Review of Their State 400 Years After the Reformation.* New York, Humanities Press.

Routley, Erik. *English Religious Dissent.* New York: Cambridge University Press, 1960.

Tavard, George H. *Protestantism,* tr. Rachel Attwater. New York: Hawthorn Books, 1959.

Vipart, E. *The Story of Quakerism through Three Centuries.* London, 1959.

Index